12 Rules for (Academic) Life

Tara Brabazon

12 Rules for (Academic) Life

A Stroppy Feminist's Guide through
Teaching, Learning, Politics, and Jordan
Peterson

 Springer

Tara Brabazon ⓘD
Flinders University
Adelaide, SA, Australia

ISBN 978-981-16-9290-1   ISBN 978-981-16-9291-8   (eBook)
https://doi.org/10.1007/978-981-16-9291-8

This Springer imprint is published by the registered company Springer Nature Singapore Pte Ltd.
The registered company address is: 152 Beach Road, #21-01/04 Gateway East, Singapore 189721,
Singapore

Dedicated to Professor Jamie Quinton
for breathing life into an old goth

Contents

Chapter 1
Introduction: Do you have skin in this game?

Academic life at the moment has a touch of an old western about it. White hats and black hats. An aggressive truth-seeking individual holds centre stage, victimized by feminist harpies and Marxists on one side. They talk of revolution. They always do. On his other side are the decadent, nasty, angry, dogmatic French postmodernists. Clever foreigners. What a nightmare. In the final scene, a noble Canadian succumbs to the emotional torture from the harpies and those verbose—if stylish—foreigners and rides off into the sunset, subsidized by donations from the Alt-Right.

Jordan Peterson presents many faces, identities, aspirations and demons. Whatever our personal views, his presence allows scholars and citizens to ask questions about fact, reality, truth, information and knowledge. Indeed, this book will ask questions about how Peterson has been able to avoid corrections to his research while upholding the imperatives of facts, reality and truth. More directly, I ask why Peterson became popular and how the supposed reality of the North American university system was imposed on the rest of the world. How did mentions of race become postmodern? How and why did a mediocre academic, from a small discipline that is not generalizable to the rest of the university sector, ignore the views of scholars with expertise far beyond his own?

I am your stroppy feminist guide through this journey. Welcome to the 12 rules for (academic) life. While reading Jordan Peterson's *12 Rules for Life*[1] feels like watching a romantic comedy on meth,[2] I trust my journey through the academic *12 rules* is as satisfying and piquant as a Sauvignon Blanc at the end of a long day. How was this book forged? Jordan Peterson was the public intellectual of and for the presidency of Donald Trump. Trump was a simulacrum president. Peterson was a simulacrum intellectual. Peterson was a middling academic, who said the unsayable, and became famous at the time the Alt-Right was in need of a white man in a suit to

---

[1] Peterson (2018a).

[2] I also note the resonance with 'twelve steps' that dominate both recovery and self-help movements.

T. Brabazon, *12 Rules for (Academic) Life*,
https://doi.org/10.1007/978-981-16-9291-8_1

show gravitas.[3] This truncated if tragic story became more concerning when Peterson started to believe his own hyperbole and was invested in self-absorbed fame rather than any pretence of knowledge.

Both Trump and Peterson were found out. At the end of their reigns, they surrounded themselves with the protective pillow of family members as they were the only support on which they could rely. Their daughters were enablers because the rest of the world had either disengaged, or was stunned, or horrified.[4] Indeed, *Matt Lewis and the News* podcast asked Peterson on March 21, 2018 if he would have voted for Trump over Clinton. Peterson stated, "I think … I would've impulsively voted for Trump at the last moment."[5] The rationale for voting for Donald Trump requires considered attention.[6] However, voting for him impulsively[7] necessitates some deeper understanding. What is happening here? The relationships between public and private, consciousness and reflexive action, intellect and emotion are, to cite and change The Smiths, oscillating wildly.[8] For all the outrage and bluster about language, law and the trans community, Jordan Peterson's YouTube account has strangely—and quietly—moved almost all his videos refusing pronouns to private mode where they can no longer be viewed by the public.

This book maintains both parameters and a purpose. The Jordan Peterson moment[9] commences on September 28, 2016, with his video "Professor against political correctness,"[10] which expressed his outrage about law, language and trans citizens. This accelerated history concludes less than three years later, on April 19, 2019 in the Sony Entertainment Centre in Toronto. On this day, Good Friday, Jordan Peterson and Slavoj Zizek debated in front of 3000 people, and a paying online audience.[11] The topic of the debate encircled happiness, Marxism and capitalism. Yes. Really. Zizek had one job. That focus is difficult for Zizek. Managing his nose is a full-time job. But Zizek had one job, and on this occasion, he achieved it. He had to demonstrate that Jordan Peterson knew nothing about Marxism or postmodernism.

---

[3] I note Lipsitz (2006). He states, "public policy and private prejudice work together to create a 'possessive investment in whiteness' that is responsible for the racialized hierarchies in our society," loc 14.

[4] Please refer to Peterson (2021a).

[5] Matt Lewis and News podcast (2018).

[6] Brabazon et al. (2018).

[7] The importance of considered and careful thinking was effectively explored through Narvaez (2010).

[8] The Smiths (1987).

[9] Tylor Lovins recognizes that Jordan Peterson's timing is important. They state, "the man has been properly situated in our cultural moment," from Peterson (2018b). This book uses 'this moment' to focus on how Jordan Peterson re-establishes the value of truth, reality and religion, and critiques evil.

[10] The original video has either been removed or rendered private. Please refer to Reddit.com (2020). Significantly, the version of the video mentioned in the Reddit feed has also been removed from YouTube. It is intriguing how this first, public moment for Jordan Peterson to express his free speech has been removed by the speaker.

[11] Lian (2019).

He succeeded. All the straw men summoned through Peterson's description of "Postmodern NeoMarxists"[12] sashayed away as the great philosophers Kansas specified, "like dust in the wind."[13] It was a poor debate. Neither were on form, and neither explored happiness.[14] But this debate was the end of Peterson as a public intellectual.[15] He was certainly public, but the intellectual component of the compound noun was destroyed by Zizek.[16]

Following this debate, a Post Peterson Paradigm emerged. As with all posts—poststructuralism, postcolonialism and postmodernism—the positioning of the prefix 'post' allows us to reflect on the word that follows. And—dear reader—there is a sickening sting in the tale of this particular post. It is very easy to chop up Jordan Peterson's ideas, like capsicum in a stir fry. It is very easy to ignore these views, because they contribute little but acid to an already burning university sector. It is also easy—and perhaps accurate—to demonstrate that Peterson's *12 Rules* are a replaying of Margaret Thatcher's "Victorian Values,"[17] summoning individuals and families and denying the capacity of societal and collective solutions. Similarly, it is simple to view Jordon Peterson as an apologist for a toxic and failed neoliberalism that nearly destroyed the international social and economic system through the Global Financial Crisis,[18] but like the White Walkers are stumbling on, to enact one more attempt at destruction.[19] It is straightforward to view Jordan Peterson as a much less skilled but much more effective replay of Alan Bloom's *The Closing of the American Mind*,[20] or Robert Bly's *Iron John*,[21] but involving lobsters.[22] It is effortless to laugh at his four most common references, the four horsemen of the zombie apocalypse: the Bible, Dostoyevsky, Solzhenitsyn and Jung. It is like referencing the four Beatles but without the music, the haircuts, the Chelsea boots, or the talent. It is like a Disney

---

[12] Peterson (2017a). I also acknowledge Tabatha Southey's definition of this term. "Postmodern neo-Marxism' ... is a conspiracy theory holding that an international cabal of Marxist academics, realizing that traditional Marxism is unlikely to triumph any time soon, is out to destroy Western civilization by undermining its cultural values with 'cultural' taken out of the name so it doesn't sound quite so similar to the literal Nazi conspiracy theory of 'cultural Bolshevism,'" *Maclean's*, November 17, 2017, Is Jordan Peterson the stupid man's smart person? - Macleans.ca.

[13] Kansas (1978).

[14] I note that Peterson was a third author on a refereed article with Burton and Plaks (2015). This study confirmed that, "neuroticism negatively correlated with conservatism," and neuroticism impacted on happiness. It is important to note the correlations in this study, not the causality.

[15] While a series of personal matters followed this event, including Tammy Peterson's illness and Jordan Peterson's addiction to benzodiazepines, this lecture was an ending to any pretence that he held intellectual expertise beyond a very small slice of research in clinical psychology. The scale of this evaporation from public discourse was captured by Lewis (2021).

[16] Michael Fedorovsky offered a commentary and review of this debate (2019). Significantly, 'intellectual' was not deployed as a noun through this article.

[17] Samuel (1992).

[18] Tett (2009).

[19] I recognize the strong research completed by Chapman et al. (2014).

[20] Bloom (1987).

[21] Bly (1992).

[22] Peterson (2018).

movie pretending to offer ontological insights after the happy ending. Such critiques are crisp and unproblematic. But there is something more here. In the pages that follow, I explore why Jordon Peterson was hot for a New York Minute.

I was reading, listening to and watching Jordan Peterson during the last few years with a combination of bored disinterest and intellectual concern. I did not want to add one citation to his record, or one more mention for Google's bots to locate. When heat and light are given to the cold, dark, disturbing and wrong, the errors can amplify. Then his wife became sick, and a Post Peterson Paradigm emerged. I realized, as will be revealed in my Rule 11, that I was one of the few people who can—with the power of experiential horror and profound loss—offer a critique of his hypocrisy. But also, I summon a living commentary about (academic) death, to offer a bitter vinaigrette of warning.

I offer twelve rules, that are not rules. They are mantras for consideration over coffee, thoughts while cleaning the house, or topics for a quiet chat with friends over a posh Savvy Blanc. I have skin in this game, but this book offers no personal attack. It is a book of argument, debate and interpretation of research. Occasionally, it is a book of negation, of refusal to sit in silence, to maintain complicity and complacency with an educational and economic system that demeans and marginalizes so many.[23] Yet it is difficult to sustain credibility as a scholar in such times. As a researcher in the humanities, but also a theorist, a scholar of Marx, an historian, a Cultural Studies academic, and a feminist, white, heterosexual woman who has not had children, I am Satan in this intellectual scrag fight. In an odd inversion of identity politics, I am stripped of scholarship. My research is parked. Instead of my words being assessed as research, I am reduced to breasts, ovaries, and a shrill feminist voice. I am Peterson's "crazy, harpy sister."[24] From this Alt-Right version of identity politics, I am everything that is wrong with international higher education. To make this situation even worse, I am an Australian. We approach every problem with an open mouth.

While my vagina may seem an intellectual anchor in any scholarly debate, discounting me from serious intellectual commentary, like the Fool in King Lear, I ask one—potent—question. How did a mediocre, Canadian clinical psychologist become famous? I have an answer to that question, and I offer it for your consideration. To begin this answer, we start with a fun fact. In the nineteenth century, there was a book that outsold Charles Darwin's *On the Origin of Species* and Karl Marx and Friedrich Engel's *The Communist Manifesto*. It was written by a man who was famous in his own lifetime. A sought-out speaker and writer, his name was Samuel Smiles. His best known and bestselling book was *Self Help*.[25] Yes, that was the title. This was the book that started the concept and the industry.

The subtitle of *Self Help*, published in 1859, was "with illustrations of conduct and perseverance." It was a book that celebrated individual men and hard work.

---

[23] Honig (2021). She argued for the collective act of refusal.

[24] Peterson (2017b).

[25] Smiles (1859).

It embraced the growth of character. Its critiques were just as precise: "the function of government is negative and restrictive, rather than positive and active."[26] Meritocracy and perseverance summon what Smiles describes as "energetic men of business."[27] It is a book of inspiration, with great man after great man (after great man) promising social mobility through self-denial, self-discipline and self-respect. Smiles confirms that "a man's character is seen in small matters."[28] Poverty is caused through the perpetuation of bad habits (obviously). To understand the starkness of argument, alongside its wrongness, it is necessary to summon its time. The book was published in 1859. The industrial revolution was pounding change through social and economic structures, resulting in desperate poverty and exploitation throughout England. Development was volatile and uneven. What possible mechanism was available to convince young men to work hard, with few opportunities for financial stability and a pleasant life?

The answer was—you are ahead of me, dear reader—self-help. Women were irrelevant to the story of great men doing great men business. Women were not required for Samuel Smiles' 'project', with only a couple of mentions of great men's wives. Great men are not distracted by women. They sacrifice and endure. The difficulty with *Self Help* is that the book is wrong. Meritocracy is an ideology.[29] Hard work does not create a decent life, because work is unstable, unpredictable and precarious. It is a lovely tale: an individual works hard and is rewarded for effort. It is, as Thomas Hughes has described it, "a version of compassionate conservatism."[30] A person of ability is valued and becomes socially mobile. These were meritocratic dreams perpetuated in the nineteenth century to stop working class men questioning their lives and collectivizing their struggles with other working-class men to create structural, social, economic and political change.

Samuel Smiles became a celebrity through *Self Help*. Once a reformer, chartist and advocate for female suffrage, he moved to a focus on individual men of humble origins who became great through thrift, denial and self-control. Jordan Peterson is the Samuel Smiles of the twenty-first century. He wrote a book about individual men working hard, struggling and taking on their responsibilities.[31] Today, we rarely hear the name Samuel Smiles. The movement he berthed discarded his legacy and focussed on the more lucrative audience of women 'having it all' and middle-class men being 'productive' in 'business.' Malcolm Gladwell has created a career based on simple answers to simple questions. Tony Robbins has forged a guru-enabled

---

[26] ibid., loc 15.

[27] ibid., loc 497.

[28] ibid., loc 3019.

[29] I note the outstanding research from Case and Deaton (2020). In this remarkable book, the researchers investigate what happens to those who 'fail' in a meritocracy. They explored the three fastest rising death rates: suicides, drug overdoses and alcoholic liver disease.

[30] Hughes (2008).

[31] In Peterson (2021b), he stated that, "If you want to become invaluable in a workplace—in any community—just do the useful things no one else is doing. Arrive earlier and leave later than your compatriots (but do not deny yourself your life)," p. 112. Here is the perpetuation of Samuel Smiles. If the worker simply workers harder, their value will be recognized by the system.

income stream by re-telling the tale of how his mother ruined his life, but like the strong man that he is, overcame these injustices and enabled millions of other people to—similarly—blame their mothers. There is an industry composed of men who tell other men to 'man up' and ensure women calm down and be quiet. As Joe Dixon argued with the subtlety of a brick through a window,

> Peterson is delighted with the patriarchy. It fills him with joy. He hates Marxism, feminism and postmodernism because they don't. He seeks to destroy anything that seeks to redistribute power. He fights on behalf of the patriarchy. It's the 'natural order,' he lyingly says. The natural order is for decrepit old power structures to fall, and be replaced. Peterson defends inheritance, privilege, anti-meritocracy, anti-competition, nepotism and cronyism—all the factors that allow the senile patriarchy to endure.[32]

Scholars must not be evangelical in their commitments. Jordan Peterson, as with so many preachers, has been found out as a hypocrite, advising others to uphold standards that he cannot reach. If the intellectual currency is faith, worship, devotion and emulation, then the intellectual deity must be worthy of such attention. Indeed, his own publishers were uncomfortable to publish the second instalment in his self-help journey, and then had to manage controversies on the grounds of quality and reputational damage.[33] Titled *Beyond Order: 12 More Rules for Life*, this book is no *Empire Strikes Back*. It is not even *The Phantom Menace*. Jordan Peterson's book is the Jar Jar Binks of scholarship. Peterson offers simple answers to questions that no one is asking. He exists to make the powerful feel both comfortable and justifiable in their power. His band aid answers do not even mask, let alone heal, the weeping wounds of injustice. North America is not ruled by "Postmodern NeoMarxists."[34] It is led by billionaire capitalists who confirm the stock market as the barometer of growth, and real estate prices as a proxy for social mobility. Instead, speculation has been conflated with economic development. Any cultural force—including stock market crashes, energy crises and a pandemic—that stops a person being able to buy toilet paper or receive a haircut at the moment of their choosing is greeted with the label of 'Marxist.'

What is the problem?

We know—don't we?—that Marxists are not the problem. Unlike Samuel Smiles, Charles Darwin, Karl Marx and Friedrich Engels remain known and discussed in our present. They wrote of histories beyond themselves. They deployed reasoning, scholarship and expertise to offer complex interpretations of the changes that have punctuated not only their lived experiences, but histories of human development. It is important to remember that the Peterson 'moment' commenced in and with a denial of trans citizens and their right to name and speak their belonging, their identity and their injustice. One of the reasons that Peterson's critique of trans rights was so successful was—and is—that scholars and citizens have lost, denied or decentred

---

[32] Dixon (2018).

[33] Behune (2021), Jordan Peterson's upcoming book has opened up a clash of values at its publisher—Macleans.ca.

[34] Peterson (2017).

the connections between self and society, identity and community, consumers and citizens.

Individuals have responsibilities. One of those responsibilities is to respect our past, but not to be rendered complacent by it. Identity is not the foundation of politics. Experience is not the foundation for justice. Instead, marginalized citizens, like women, have been labelled and judged and minimized when oppressing others. Yes, 'Karens' can be a problem. TERFs are a challenge. But with the focus on Karens and TERFs, Jordan Petersons proliferate and populate populism with ill-informed, insular opinion.[35] There are other ways to organize knowledge, meaning and community. When injustice is ranked in a hierarchy of experience, then the empowered maintain their power. An easy politics emerges with the question, 'What do we stand for?' Life experience and anecdotes can answer that question. A tougher question, for difficult times, is how much injustice can we as citizens stand? How many injustices do we walk past and accept? Such questions require research, arching beyond our singular life narrative. The injustices confronting First Nations Peoples, children, the elderly, citizens with impairments, the unemployed, the underemployed, those in poverty, the homeless, women, intersexual, transgender and non binary identifying folk are all distinctive,[36] but by building connections, communicating and creating coalition-building discussions for new modes of community, alternative ways of living can be summoned. New modes of belonging, listening and living can be created.[37] Labelling a Karen[38] or a TERF[39] is an easy act from a keyboard warrior. Taking the time to build affinities, consciousness and conversation is more difficult but also sustains and enables political imperatives for change.

Elise Meyer provides a model and framework for this mode of thinking.[40] She probes the "indeterminacy" of the word "woman" in the Convention on the

---

[35] I remain inspired by Olufemi (2020). She affirms the value of a feminism "of questioning," p. 4. She also logs "the pressure to 'do' gender correctly," p. 55. This book is a reminder that women's oppression is caused and perpetuated by many forces and ideologies beyond biological determinism. For Olufemi, feminism is a space to consider and configure liberation.

[36] The challenge politically remains how to value and validate different histories and experiences, while also building collaborations, partnerships and affinities to activate social, cultural and economic change. I particularly note Barker and Iantaffi's research (2020). They enact the intricate theoretical and historical work to understand the differences between the non binary identifying citizens and trans citizens. They show how the 'cis' and 'trans' binary may create additional challenges. Transwomen are women. Transmen are men. Recognizing the key research by Gayle Rubin, they demonstrate how binary models of 'orientation' are part of the colonial project of categorizing different people and creating a hierarchy of humans. They also ask the important question: who gains from creating sharp binaries of straight and gay, cis and trans, male and female?

[37] I note the outstanding edited collection from Crimmins (2019).

[38] 'Karens' describe an irritating and entitled white woman. Particularly through COVID-19, Karens proliferated through memes and popular culture. Please refer to: Nagesh (2020), Wong (2020), and Tiffany (2020).

[39] TERF refers to a Trans Exclusive Radical Feminist. The volume and heat of this debate is captured by Pearce et al. (2020). They stated, "We have not sought out the TERF wars; rather, the TERF wars have found us," and they confirm the strong affinities and partnerships between the trans and feminist communities, noting the plural history of both.

[40] Meyer (2016).

Elimination of all forms of discrimination against women (CEDAW). She works through reproductive capacity, anatomy, genetics, socialization, history and geography. Therefore, 'trans' captures a socialization, a variation from ideological norms and expectations. The reason for this variability is that dominant gender behaviours, languages and performances are so diverse. Hugh Ryan confirmed that the term 'trans' is used to "capture all the identities—from drag queen to genderqueer—that fall outside traditional gender norms."[41] If the focus remains on human rights, then a refocussing through the lens of justice, injustice, discrimination, marginalization and in/equality offers new trajectories for dialogue and conversations. This is the Judith Butler project: "to undo restrictively normative conceptions of sexual and gendered life."[42] The outcome of such a project is to render our lives meaningful, thoughtful, conscious, purposeful, and shared.

Ponder a triangle to consider how identity, consciousness and meaning is constructed.

These three variables are not linear or progressive. A simple narrative may seem to align desire, behaviour and identity. Yet these three variables rarely cluster or mesh. To provide one example from Morty Diamond:

> When I became a transman (Female-to-male transexual), my frame of reference regarding mutual attraction and having a love life changed drastically. Formerly dyke-identified, as I worked to understand and reformulate my new gender identity, I figured I could throw everything I learned about finding sex and love as a woman out the window … I wasn't quite sure who was going to date me.[43]

The indeterminacy of Diamond's testimony is important. Behaviour, desire and identity are not consistent, but subjective, historical and are not publicly available for scrutiny. These are personal thoughts that may or may not manifest into public language, affirmations and behaviours. As Dara Hoffman-Fox has shown, the expectations of gender create uncertainty and fear.[44] The terms like trans, intergender,

---

[41] Ryan (2014).

[42] Butler (2004).

[43] Diamond (2011).

[44] Hoffman-Fox (2017).

genderfluid, gender queer, transmale and transfemale capture the complexity of consciousness development.

Working through the relationship between the personal and the political has been the central project of the feminist movement.[45] Feminism sits in and with contradictions. Errors, inaccuracies and mistakes are made by feminist scholars, like all scholars from diverse paradigms and theoretical perspectives.[46] But it is important to remember the scholarly career of Dorothy Smith. She affirmed the "standpoint of women."[47]

> 'Standpoint' as the design of a subject position in institutional ethnography creates a point of entry into discovering the social that does not subordinate the knowing subject to objectified forms of knowledge of society or political economy.[48]

Other words are used to describe a 'standpoint.' It may be positionality or a lens. But the lens configured in this book—from a heterosexual, white woman—is not exclusive of other standpoints. I welcome the lens that readers will offer that is different, provocative and powerful. All knowledge is situated. Welcome to my situation. I hope you will welcome me to your situation. Let us communicate and build communities of knowing, thinking and listening, rather than assuming, ignoring and talking.

This book summons an agenda. Therefore, this book, inspired by bell hooks, not only recognizes "strategic essentialism,"[49] but strategic binarism. I use the binaries. I play with them. I bend them. I laugh at them. Similarly, I understand and name white privilege and claim responsibility for the colonization that undergirds and structures our present. I know the strengths and the challenges of being a heterosexual woman. I use the empowerment to enter a debate about heterosexual empowerment. I deploy the injustices and marginalization. I recognize the exclusions, the confusions and the complexities. But I lean towards the challenges. There are no happy endings. There are no easy answers to simple questions. Situated knowledges operate against positivist science.[50]

At the moment, we have a Punch and Judy Show in action, where Jordan Peterson playfights with TERFs and Karens. I have watched these circus performances suck the heat and the light of attention while economic injustice, environmental destruction and a global pandemic scarred our body politic. I choose to leave the circus and follow different narratives. To summon the inspirational Raewyn Connell, a researcher who has offered profound interpretations through my professional life, "noticing gender is easy, understanding it is a great challenge."[51] In this book, let us accept this challenge. Listen. Think. Ponder arguments. Read footnotes. Track research. Let us learn from

---

[45] Hartsock (2019).
[46] Frances-White (2018).
[47] Smith (1987).
[48] Smith (2005).
[49] Hooks (1991).
[50] Lykke (2010).
[51] Connell (2021).

Jordan Peterson and this Punch and Judy moment of academic populism. We can do better than this.

In our accelerated lives, Jordan Peterson's Samuel Smiles moment lasted three years. His moment is over. But as with Smiles, we need to understand why this moment required a man telling other men to pull up their bootstraps. Therefore, let us move to the rules, some mantras for your consideration.

References

Behune, B. (2021). Jordan Peterson's upcoming book has opened up a lash of values at its publisher. *Maclean's*. Retrieved February 25, 2021.

Bloom, A. (1987). *The closing of the American mind*. Penguin Books.

Bly, R. (1992). *Iron John*. Dorset and Rockport.

Brabazon, T., Redhead, S., & Chivaura, R. (2018). *Trump Studies; why citizens vote against their interests*. Bingley.

Barker, M. J., & Iantaffi, A. (2020). *Life isn't binary: On being both, beyond, and in-between.*. Jessica Kingsley Publishers.

Burton, C. M., & Plaks, J. E. (2015). Why do conservatives report being happier than liberals? The contribution to neuroticism.*Psych Open*, *3*(1). https://jspp.psychopen.eu/index.php/jspp/article/view/4839.

Butler, J. (2004). *Undoing gender* (p. 23). Routledge.

Case, A., & Deaton, A. (2020). *Deaths of despair and the future of capitalism*. Princeton University Press.

Chapman, G., White, P., & Myra, H. (2014). *Rising above the toxic workplace*. Northfield Publishing.

Connell, R. (2021). *Gender in world perspectives* (p. 147). Polity.

Crimmins, G. (2019). *Strategies for resisting sexism in the academy: Higher education, gender and intersectionality*. Palgrave.

Diamond, M. (2011). Embodiment of love. In: Diamond, M. (Ed). *Radical sex, love, and relationships beyond the gender binary* (p. 66). Manic D Press

Dixon, J. (2018). *Clean up your room! The eternal spotless mind of Jordan Peterson* (p. 693). Self-published

Frances-White, D. (2018). *The Guilty feminist: From our noble goals to our worst hypocrisies*. Virago.

Fedorovsky, M. The debate between Slavoj Zizek and Jordan Peterson. *Dialektika, 1*(1), 38–44.

Hartsock, N. (2019). *The feminist standpoint revisited and other essays*. Routledge.

Honig, B. (2021). *A feminist theory of refusal*. Harvard University Press.

Hoffman-Fox, D. (2017). *You and your gender identity: A guide to discovery*. Skyhorse publishing.

Hooks, B. (1991). Essentialism and experience. *American Literary History*, *3*(1), 172–183.

Hughes, T. (2008). Retroview: in his proper place. *The American Interest*, *1*(1).

Kansas. (1978). Dust in the wind. In: *Point of no return*. Kirshner.

Lewis, H. (2021). What happened to Jordan Peterson? *The Atlantic*.

Lipsitz, G. (2006). *The possessive investment in whiteness*. Temple University.

Lian, A. (2019). The Toronto debate: Jordan Peterson and Slavoj Zizek on ethics and happiness. *The European Legacy, 24*(6), 644–650.

Lykke, N. (2010). *Feminist studies: A guide to intersectional theory, methodology and writing*. Routledge.

Matt Lewis and the News podcast. (2018). Jordan Peterson. Retrieved March 21, 2018, from https://www.mattklewis.com/matt-lewis-and-the-news/jordan-peterson/

Meyer, E. (2016). Designing women: The definition of 'woman' in the convention on the elimination of all forms of discrimination against women. *Chicago Journal of International Law, 16*(2), 553–590.

Nagesh, A. (2020). What exactly is a 'Karen' and where did the meme come from? *BBC News*. Retrieved July 30, 2020, from https://www.bbc.com/news/world-53588201

Narvaez, D. (2010). Moral complexity: The fatal attraction of truthiness and the importance of mature moral functioning. *Perspectives on Psychological Science, 5*(2), 163–181.

Olufemi, L. (2020). *Feminism, interrupted: disrupting power*. Pluto.

Pearce, R., Erikainen, S., & Vincent, B. (2020). TERF wars: An introduction. *The Sociological Review, 68*(4), 677–698.

Peterson, J. (2017a). Postmodern Neomarxism: Diagnosis and cure. *YouTube*. Retrieved July 10, 2017, from https://www.youtube.com/watch?v=s4c-jOdPTN8.

Peterson, J. (2017b). Modern Times with Camille Paglia and Jordan Peterson. *YouTube*. Retrieved October 3, 2017, from https://www.youtube.com/watch?v=v-hIVnmUdXM.

Peterson, J. (2018a). *12 Rules for Life: An antidote for chaos*. Penguin.

Peterson, J. B. (2018b). The man has been properly situated in our cultural moment. In: *Why tell the Truth: An introduction to the basic ideas of Jordan B. Peterson* (p. 13). Self-published.

Peterson, J. (2021b). *12 More rules for life* (p. 111). Penguin.

Peterson, M. (2021a). Mikhaila Peterson: How we built the Jordan Peterson media empire. *National Post*. Retrieved March 1, 2021, from https://nationalpost.com/news/canada/mikhaila-peterson-how-we-built-the-jordan-peterson-media-empire

Reddit.com. (2020). Professor against political correctness. *Reddit.com*. Retrieved August 3, 2020, from https://www.reddit.com/r/JordanPeterson/comments/i2k3kj/professor_against_political_correctness/

Ryan, H. (2014). What does trans* mean and where did it come from. *SLATE*. Retrieved January 10, 2014, from http://www.slate.com/blogs/outward/2014/01/10/trans_what_does_it_mean_and_where_did_it_come_from

Samuel, R. (1992). Mrs Thatcher's return to victorian values. *Proceedings of the British Academy, 78*, 9–29. http://publications.thebritishacademy.ac.uk/pubs/proc/files/78p009.pdf

Smiles, S. (1859). *Self-Help; with illustrations of conduct and perseverance*. Oxford World.

Smith, D. (1987). *The everyday world as problematic: A feminist sociology*. Northeastern University Press.

Smith, D. (2005). *Institutional ethnography: A sociology for people* (p. 10). Roman & Littlefield.

Trump, I. (2022). Ivanka Trump tweets. https://twitter.com/IvankaTrump

The Smiths. (1987). Oscillate wildly. *Louder than Bombs* (p. 15). Rough Trade.

Tett, G. (2009). *Fool's Gold: How unrestrained greed corrupted a dream, shattered global markets and unleashed a catastrophe*. Little, Brown.

Tiffany, K. (2020). How 'Karen' became a Coronavirus villain. *The Atlantic*. Retrieved May 6, 2020, from https://www.theatlantic.com/technology/archive/2020/05/coronavirus-karen-memes-reddit-twitter-carolyn-goodman/611104/

Wong, J. (2020). The year of Karen: how a meme changed the way Americans talked about racism. *The Guardian*. Retrieved December 27, 2020, from https://www.theguardian.com/world/2020/dec/27/karen-race-white-women-black-americans-racism

Chapter 2
Rule 1–Always Ask Why

New phrases jut from our complicated present. Innovative tropes. Transgressive theories. Provocative slogans. Uncomfortable information. Defiant knowledge. Difficult (post)disciplines.

Trump Studies. Sports Humanities. Physical Cultural Studies. Deviant Leisure. Extreme Anthropology. Ultra Realist Criminology. Brexit Criminology. Post Digital Studies.

Such terms and phrases open red wedges, disruptive arguments, and dangerous intellectual opportunities. These phrases have tumbled from the last decade of university history as the global left attached themselves to 'theory' and 'theorists.' The celebrity intellectual culture, which developed through the 2000s, produced open access online journals devoted to theorists such as Jean Baudrillard and Slavoj Zizek. This is open knowledge in a time of commercialized research.[1] These journals and

---

[1] Academic publishing is complex. It can be highly corporatized, with Springer and Elsevier maintaining large profit margins. But open access is important to this conversation, and it is relevant to Jordan Peterson's publishing 'choices.' There are tiers of Open Access Publishing. Platinum Open Access is a status confirmed when neither the author nor the reader pays anything for access to research. These journals are listed and easily located on the Directory of Open Access Journals, www.doaj.org. Therefore, there is an academic space that exists outside of the commercial academic publishers, and the contributory businesses that make academic authors pay for Open Access. Yet Jordan Peterson's 'publishing' operates differently, based on a mis-configuration of academic publishing. His daughter stated that they, "provide easy access to his ideas for anyone who is interested in hearing them—without hiding them behind a paywall (unlike universities and colleges). Advertising allows us to keep his ideas free," from Peterson (2021). This is a clear presentation of the neoliberal university. Supposedly, higher education keeps the ideas of scholars behind 'paywalls.' But advertising allows the material to be 'free.' Such a simplistic statement blocks the presentation of the reality. Universities create free repositories for open access research, featuring pre-print versions of articles to ensure that the research remains available to citizens. This is not about individual academics making choices. Nations and trans-national communities have committed to open access. Please refer to "Open Access," European Commission, March 2020, https://ec.europa.eu/info/research-and-innovation/strategy/goals-research-and-innovation-policy/open-science/open-access_en.

T. Brabazon, *12 Rules for (Academic) Life*,
https://doi.org/10.1007/978-981-16-9291-8_2

projects render unstable corporate publishers and traditional methodologies, often limited by empiricism.

This instability matters. This is an interregnum.[2] In its historical and science fictional manifestations, an interregnum is a gap, a break or an aperture in governmental organization and social order. Originally used to describe the space between the reigns of monarchs, the word also captured the social unrest in these periods, invoking succession wars or foreign invasions. Failed states jut from interregna. Antonio Gramsci's interregnum was much more precisely constituted, emerging from his writing about the 'crisis' in late 1920s and early 1930s Italy. These periods are characterized by a suspension of expectations and a parking of future hopes. In such a moment, the powerful frequently deploy violence to sustain some mode of order. It is not a surprise that Zygmunt Bauman found resonance and value in Gramsci's interregnum and summoned the concept to probe the period of globalization and financial crises.[3]

Therefore, in our interregnum, we return to Trump Studies. Sports Humanities. Physical Cultural Studies. Post Digital Studies. Deviant Leisure. Extreme Anthropology. Ultra Realist Criminology. Post Digital Studies. This stroppy, potent knowledge is not budding from the Ivy League, Russell Group or the Group of Eight universities. Instead, this dangerous knowledge is pulsating from unstable, daring institutions. Deviant Leisure emerged from Plymouth University. Ultra Realist Criminology sprang from Teesside University and now resides at Northumbria. Extreme Anthropology originated from Oslo. Physical Cultural Studies bolted from Waikato, Bath, Bournemouth and Maryland. Sports Humanities emerged from Waseda. Post Digital Studies comes from Coventry University. This is not centred and safe knowledge. This is discourse from the edges. It is pervasive and promiscuous knowledge that does not abide by disciplinary rules. It is not only highly theoretical but anti-empirical. Its relationship with science, and scientific methods, is similarly critical.

In Theoretical Times,[4] it may seem lithe and glib to affirm the freedom of speech. But is there a line, a barrier or demarcation that we cannot cross? Put another way—and more directly—do you believe anyone has the right to say anything to anybody? Is that a freedom? Is that a fighting freedom? One definition of life is the management of disappointments. Political and public debates emerge when determining where that personal disappointment is lodged and how i tis expressed. If disappointment creates self-awareness and knowledge, then it can lead to a quest for self-improvement and learning. If these disappointments are blamed on the presence of others—such as migrants, the young, the old, the gay community or women—then the resultant oppressions are damaging to individuals and corrosive to any form of consensus building that may improve health, housing, education or the working life for the majority of citizens.[5] At what point does the celebration of an individual's strength of

---

[2] To view my reading of this interregnum, outside of this research monograph, please refer to Brabazon et al. (2018).

[3] Bauman (2012).

[4] Redhead (2017).

[5] Campbell (2011).

views result in destructive fragmentation? This empowered, volatile, righteous, self-absorbed individual has a history. It did not emerge - or die - through the presidency of Donald Trump.

Scholars require new, radical, edgy and passionate methodologies, epistemologies and ontologies to engage with this social, cultural, economic and intellectual maelstrom, without resorting to glib cliches like "Believe the Science" or "Freedom of Speech."[6] Both these phrases are the slogans of the desperate, who have not completed the complex foundational work to formulate the information literacy to understand the science, or the reflexive consciousness to realize that personal rights are not of greater value or importance than collective rights. This is, as Carl Bergstrom and Jevin West have confirmed, a confusion between the attention economy and information literacy.[7] It is also a misunderstanding of research methodology. Data are just data. Measurements may not be accurate. Random samples may be - to summon the hashtag - #random and therefore not generalizable or representative. That which is false is often believed because it is simpler than the true and the verifiable.

Instead of these complex and difficult tasks of learning, reading and thinking, the volatility, agitation and weirdness within the political landscape is clear. Jordan Peterson uploads a video. Donald Trump used to tweet, before he was reported for inciting violence through his words.[8] These movements are operating in a space where scholars and scholarship are frequently silent, decentred and denied. Perhaps silenced is a more precise verb. Is this disconnection between politics and scholarship a recognition that 'experts' have failed to move—to cite Antonio Gramsci—from common sense to good sense? It is the time to reverse such a trend. It is the time to understand why Jordan Peterson exists. It is time to ask why.

Populism and popular culture are distinct entities. Jordan Peterson is part of popular culture, but has used populist methods to get there.[9] Popular culture is not benevolent. Progressives may wish for the creation and perpetuation of a feminist,

---

[6] This evangelical 'belief' in science was demonstrated in a letter to the editor from seven professors to New Zealand's *Listener* magazine. These professors 'defended' science against Matauranga Maori. Please refer to Clements et al. (2021). In response to this letter, the Vice Chancellor of the University of Auckland expressed her concerns with the content of the letter and over 2000 academics confirmed the scientific value of Matauranga Maori. Georgina Tuari Stewart wrote a powerful response to this letter and the subsequent debate. She stated that, "it is relatively rare for seven senior professors, mostly of science, to publish a letter to the Editor of the *Listener*. The volume and general quality of the ensuing debate could well leave the average citizen unconvinced: surely senior professors at the biggest, most prestigious university in the country know what they are talking about? The principles of freedom of speech and academic freedom underwrite the right of the seven professors to publish their opinion on the relationship between science and Maori knowledge. While I and others worked away over the years on the development of Maori-medium science education curriculum and assessment resources, it never occurred to us that others might pluck a few of our words out of context and use them in such antithetical, uninformed ways, absent of all ethical care, to no apparent good end. There are real threats to science in the world, but Maori knowledge is not one of them," from Tuari Stewart (2021).

[7] Berstrom and West (2020).

[8] Twitter Inc (2021).

[9] I acknowledge Benjamin Dueck's remarkable research in this area. Please refer to Dueck (2019).

vegan popular culture. Very often, popular culture is offensive, confronting, weird or disturbing. There is also what I have described as Thinking Pop,[10] or high popular culture,[11] that allows reflection on difficult issues. Thinking pop is rare, special and spectacular. Populism is distinct. It holds particular characteristics. It is critical of identity politics, while actually using its tropes, language and methodologies to deny the space and histories of the disempowered. It is critical of 'elites' that are never named or specified with precision, and it is anti-pluralist. Populism summons a morality where there is no mitigating step required for representative politics. Because 'the people'—or 'everyone' - want 'boys to be boys' or women to return to the home, this populist view is constructed and perpetuated without any evidence or debate. It is not the dominant view. It is not the majority view. It has not been verified by longitudinal studies. Instead, it provides easy answers to uncomfortable questions about men, women, work, power and the contemporary family. In other words, populism is a direct critique of representative politics. For Jordan Peterson, YouTube views, likes and comments are a substitute for a representative, democratic engagement and a vote on his ideas. Indeed, the assumptions of populism actively block the connection with the democratic process.[12] One of the consequences of the rise of unchecked populism without clear definitions and separations from popular culture is the enabling slogan of ignorance: "fake news." The capacity of the empowered to simply deny their empowerment, to pretend to represent 'the people' is the archetypal characteristic of populism. This is not popular culture. This is populism. We need to be clear on the differentiation.

Democracy is based on the majority of a population voting for representatives who conduct politics in a way that 'represents' the people. If they fail to do so, then they are removed from office. There is accountability. Populist leaders do not require a mitigating stage of representation, no matter how flawed the proxies or process. They 'represent' the people without evidence or verification. To view the confusion, it is only necessary to remember the chaos of December 2020 and January 2021 in the United States of America. Donald Trump lost the election. He did not receive the majority of votes. He did not win the electoral college. Yet the multiple attempts to deny this result—deny representative democracy—was a strategy to replace popular culture with populism. That is, removing the mitigating step of representative democracy from the creation of a government. This is the context in which Jordan Peterson emerged, fired and declined, where young men are the global citizenry, and clinical psychology is a discipline that is generalizable to all other knowledge systems. Significantly, in this interregnum, between the loss of the old order and the pause before the bloom of the new, Peterson was the scholar of choice for the empowered that were frightened of losing their power. This was a transitory status: the populist interregnum intellectual. Such notoriety has passed, as the interregnum is squeezed into a future of despair and confusion, birthed through a combination of recession,

---

[10] Brabazon (2008).

[11] Brabazon and Redhead (2015).

[12] I recognized Jan-Werner Muller's remarkable monograph (2016).

uneven un/employment, underemployment, COVID crises, COVID denial,[13] climate change, water and food security, and mediocre (at best) governmental leaders.

Put another way, Jordan Peterson does not matter. Why he gained profile and popularity—does. To focus on 'the why' enables the summoning of a different future. To remain fixated in 'the how' and 'the what' hooks us into a present where 'the people' are summoned with flourish, but denied rights to speak, manage reproduction, occupy space or—in the case of George Floyd—even breathe. Citizens are inconvenient. They speak. They answer back through their bodies and minds, their laughter and their tweets. Populism controls the plurality of citizens by denial. Popular culture offers a frequently inconvenient reminder that citizens will not behave as the dominant life narratives of work, gender, families and personal control construct for them. From that defiant spark of difference, the resultant, messy and inconvenient questioning of 'why' can be energizing and momentous.

References

Bauman, Z. (2012). Times of Interregnum. *Ethics and Global Politics, 5*(1), 49–56.

Berstrom, C., & West, J. (2020). *Calling bullshit: The art of scepticism in a data-driven world.* Penguin

Brabazon, T., Redhead, S., & Chivaura, R. (2018). *Trump studies.* Emerald.

Brabazon, T. (2008). *Thinking pop.* Ashgate.

Brabazon, T., & Redhead, S. (2015) Doctor Who: High popular culture for difficult times. *Tara Brabazon Podcast.* December 11, 2015. https://traffic.libsyn.com/secure/tarabrabazon/Doctor_Who_-_high_popular_culture_for_difficult_times.mp3

Campbell, C. (2011). *Scapegoat: A history of blaming other people.* Duckworth Overlook

Clements, K., Cooper, G., Corballis, M., Elliffe, D., Nola, R., Rata, E., & Weery, J. (2021). In defence of science. *Listener*:4

Dueck, B. (2019). Fighting back against an imaginary evil: how studying Jordan Peterson's rhetoric helps us to recognize populism in the digital age. *Crossings*(3). http://crossings.uwinnipeg.ca/index.php/crossings/article/view/114.

Muller, J. W. (2016). *What is populism?.* University of Pennsylvania Press.

Peterson, M. (2021). How we built the Jordan Peterson media empire. *National Post.* March 1, 2021. https://nationalpost.com/news/canada/mikhaila-peterson-how-we-built-the-jordan-peterson-media-empire

Redhead, S. (2017). *Theoretical Times.* Emerald.

Tuari Stewart, G. (2021). Defending science from what? *Educational Philosophy and Theory.* https://doi.org/10.1080/00131857.2021.1966415

Twitter Inc, Suspension, *Twitter.* Retrieved Jan 8, 2021, from https://blog.twitter.com/en_us/topics/company/2020/suspension.html

Zizek, S. (2020). *Panic: Covid-19 shakes the world.* Polity.

---

[13] Slavoj Zizek's question is a powerful one: "What is wrong with our system that we were caught unprepared by the catastrophe [Covid] despite scientists warning us about it for years?" This question comes from Zizek (2020).

Chapter 3
Rule 2–Be an Intellectual and make your choices about the mode

Jordan Peterson was described by the *New York Times* as "the most influential public intellectual in the world."[1] Let us take the *New York Times* as accurate for a moment. Certainly, the word 'intellectual' is flung about with the regularity of pellets in a hen house. The noun 'intellectual' also has some complex adjectives placed in front of it: public intellectual, critical intellectual and organic intellectual. All of these adjectives summon different attributes, audiences and interfaces. One interpretation of the differences is that the public intellectual participates in consensual knowledge generation and the critical intellectual offers alternative knowledge systems, challenging the status quo. Of a different order is the organic intellectual. Put another way and with examples, status quo scholars are public intellectuals such as Jordan Peterson, Alan Bloom, Henry Kissinger or Camille Paglia. Critical intellectuals summon an alternative worldview, vista or pathway. The clearest and most inspirational example was Edward Said, with Noam Chomsky and Howard Zinn being strong contenders.

From these parameters, what is the organic intellectual? The term is derived from Antonio Gramsci and his *Prison Notebooks*. This prison was not metaphoric. Gramsci was incarcerated by the Mussolini regime. Therefore, within his time, validating the status quo or summoning alternative perspectives was not sufficient to connect his past, present and future. From this setting, Gramsci configured the organic intellectual as the antithesis to the disinterested scholar, contributing methodically to an academic discipline. Gramsci critiqued the traditional notions of the intellectual as a person who holds universal reason and general truths, arguing that such a traditional intellectual maintains the status quo and reinforces existing power structures and social inequalities. In other words, this is the public intellectual. Gramsci argued that the unspoken purpose of such intellectual activity was to reproduce injustice. It is important to note that as we teach and write each day, we do not wake up in the morning and repeat the mantra, what can I do to reinforce capitalism and the patriarchy today? Intention and conscious reinforcement of the status quo are not required. If we work within the system and do not probe its injustices, we confirm

---

[1] Brooks (2018).

the status quo. The argument from Gramsci is that public intellectuals are pivotal to maintaining homogeneity, consensus and rationality, to block the consideration of hard alternatives.

To be part of a university—to be a public intellectual—we must fulfil our role, use the terminology of our disciplines, and either become or bow to the gatekeepers who patrol what is part of (or excluded from) knowledge. Ponder our PhD students. We ask them to create an original contribution to knowledge. This original contribution emerges when they conduct a literature review, which 'reviews' already existing knowledge, use agreed on, tested and repeatable methods, and extend knowledge just a bit. But what if the literature was wrong? What if the wrong questions are being asked? What if we are simply providing the knowledge that the powerful— the funders—and the grants agencies want us to discover? So much of traditional education is repetitive, cumulative, coordinating and controlling, with the imperative to perpetuate existing ideas without testing and verification. It creates common sense, insiders and outsiders. The organic intellectual is different. It is an unstable identity and contingent. It is not a comfortable positioning from which to research. Organic intellectuals move into spaces rarely considered to house knowledge. They live between groups. Their identity is relative, liminal and perilous. Gramsci argues that so much of education—learning—involves repetition, accumulation and control of current and new ideas. Teaching—generation after generation—reinforces this repetitive and commonsensical knowledge. For Gramsci, education must be more. It is disruptive. It challenges the status quo. The organic intellectual starts to research, challenge and configure uncommon sense.

The role of the organic intellectual is to show that the truths that we take for granted right now need to be justified, explained and revealed, rather than assumed. Class-based inequality must be seen and discussed, rather than assume that class always exists, and manifests in the same way through time. It is timely to remember the remarkable statement by that inspirational, confronting, and often wrong, critical and organic intellectual EP Thompson:

> The working class did not rise like the sun at an appointed time. It was present at its own making ... I do not see class as a "structure," nor even as a "category," but as something which in fact happens (and can be shown to have happened) in human relationships.[2]

With resonance to Marx and Engels, life determines consciousness. Consciousness does not determine life.[3] Why are black men in jail in numbers beyond white men? Complex answers are required to this question and those commentaries must be seen, discussed, evaluated and analysed, rather than assuming that—inevitably— that reality just 'happens.' The horror of George Floyd's death means that the status quo scholar cannot continue with a traditional law and order agenda. Classic criminology—status quo criminology—has been challenged by critical criminology. But then, the emergence of ultra realist criminology, led by Simon Winlow and Steve Hall

---

[2] Thompson (1968).

[3] Marx and Engels (2001).

and continued by the deviant leisure scholars Oliver Smith and Thomas Raymen, shattered one lens and created another, with the focus on the criminological capacities of capitalism.[4]

The organic intellectual is a maker and a communicator, intervening in practice and theory. The organic intellectual suspends common sense and reveals the provisional nature of the truths, the rules, the theories, and the histories we take for granted. Indeed, the stories we tell ourselves—and the histories that are published and read outside of the peer reviewed literature—are normative and normalizing. They are rarely densely descriptive or achingly analytical. Therefore, it requires considered strategies to intervene in the narratives we have believed all our lives. Jordan Peterson restates these stories, finding comfort in men and women performing predictable rituals in public and private space. For example, in a Tweet that shadowboxes imagined women making artificial and arbitrary choices, Jordan Peterson writes,

> I've spoken to many young women who believe their careers will be the most crucial thing in their life. Very few 30-year-old-women think that because they realize the consequences of what that entails; 60–70 hour work weeks, etc.[5]

Tweets do not permit footnotes or verification. The populist description of 'many young women' is the only evidence required by Peterson. Those individuals and communities that do not fit these structures and binaries are either ignored, demeaned or attacked, often with the justification of free speech. To summon the organic intellectual is to spend time thinking about communication systems and interface management. An organic intellectual is an expert and knows their field well, but is not satisfied simply staying in their knowledge system and talking with colleagues in their discipline. They know their field so well that they have the capacity to translate and transform that research for the wider citizenry. The research can travel, move, morph, inspire and transform. It becomes useable research. The burden is on us as scholars to reach the highest standards of scholarly work. That is the first step. But then, we must know so much that research is disseminated in a way that is contextually appropriate, rigorous, timely, but also meaningful for the citizens that fund our research. If we do this well, then research can offer timely information for people to consider when creating their view on an issue.

I am not suggesting that academics deny being academics, that we do not use our specialist language. We need to be precise. That is how knowledge is created. But I ask that we think about dissemination. We have a plan for the audiences of our research. We write to be read. Digitization gives scholars great subtlety and care in interface management. Through open access channels, journalism, podcasts and videos, scholars can find new strategies to connect research to people who can use it. If we choose and use the interfaces effectively, our research can move between the traditional, critical and organic intellectual. Most of us stay in the traditional mode. That is where the funding, citations and credibility are located. The critical

---

[4] I note the master work in this field: Winlow et al. (2017).

[5] Peterson (2021).

intellectual is a tough path, with the instability of Howard Zinn's position at Boston University being a warning about the troubled institutional boulders that topple on top of scholars who question the power of the powerful. The organic intellectuals are rare and precious. Professor Cornell West is one such intellectual, writing revelatory scholarship, working in rap, providing expertise for CNN and other media channels, but also communicating with community organizations in video and sound. Another profound example is the great Professor Marcia Langton. *Well I heard it on the radio and I saw it on the television*[6] was a transformative moment in Australian intellectual culture. That short book changed Australia, shifted the humanities, and was a first step - a first moment - of deep confrontation, and deep reflection about decolonization. Life determines consciousness.

Scholars can move between these categories of intellectual if they maintain two attributes: expertise and courage. Jordan Peterson is a status quo scholar. He is a clinical psychologist, a phrase used in his media introductions like a trophy. It is intriguing that clinical psychology is configured as a generalizable discipline that can offer commentary and modelling throughout the university.[7] It is a small intellectual area, with very different methodologies, epistemologies and ontologies from most of the arts and sciences. Clinical psychology is a very new discipline, with origins dating from 1896 through the opening of a psychology clinic at the University of Pennsylvania. The focus for the first fifty years of its history was assessment rather than treatment. There are still clinical psychology degrees that offer subjects in abnormal psychology. Therefore, the discipline is founded on clinically-based knowledge: individual's narratives, stories, issues, assessments and treatments.[8]

Jordan Peterson tells stories of individuals from his clinical practice, as if the single data point is meaningful. But then, the knight's move emerges. The clinical psychologist then jumps to the macro: the archetypes, the labels and assessments, and the treatment. Therefore, it is no surprise that Peterson focuses on individual and families, then expands to myths and archetypes. That jump is not justifiable methodologically, ontologically or epistemologically. Certainly, clinical psychology is a fine discipline with over a century of scholarship. But the methodology—as with many clinical methodologies—is a status quo mode of scholarship. The goal is to render patients normal, within the parameters of historical archetypes. It is focused on individual assessment and treatment.

It is tough to create spaces for the critical intellectual, let alone the organic intellectual. Instead, conservative and traditional ideas move through the media. Jordan Peterson is a Canadian version of Doctor Phil. He does not need Oprah. He has

---

[6] Langton (1993).

[7] For example, Xu and Peterson (2017).

[8] Indeed, Peterson (2013).

YouTube.[9] Therefore Jordan Peterson is a public intellectual, conveying the importance and value of being a normal, heterosexual and productive family man. He enacts this project outside of peer review and via disintermediated media.[10]

The organic intellectual task—if we choose to accept it—is different. The goal is to move between these categories of public, critical and organic intellectual, with consciousness. The organic intellectual uses popular culture to translate research for different audiences, translating common sense into good sense, and to fight populism by thinking deeply about the nature of popular culture. Working between popular and unpopular culture, broadcasting and narrowcasting, and understanding the three Ds - digitization, disintermediation and deterritorialization[11] - opens a ripe and potent space for the organic intellectual. If we do not enter this space, then Donald Trumps will continue to appear. Jordan Petersons will continue to appear. We need to risk—we need to occupy—un/popular culture in populist times.

References

Brabazon, T. (2014). The disintermediated librarian. *Australian Library Journal.* http://www.tandfonline.com/doi/abs/10.1080/00049670.2014.932681#.U-dpIfldWa9

Brooks, D. (2018). The Jordan Peterson Moment. *New York Times.* January 25, 2018. https://www.nytimes.com/2018/01/25/opinion/jordan-peterson-moment.html

Langton, M. (1993). *"Well, I heard it on the radio and I saw it on the television": An essay for the Australian Film Commission on the politics and aesthetics of filmmaking by and about Aboriginal people and things.* Australian Film Commission.

Lewis, H. (2021). What happened to Jordan Peterson? *The Atlantic.*https://www.theatlantic.com/magazine/archive/2021/04/what-happened-to-jordan-peterson/618082/

Marx, K., & Engels, F. (2001). *The German ideology.* International Publishers

Mar, R. A. (2013). Personal narratives as the highest level of cognitive integration. *Behavioural and Brain Sciences, 36*(3), 216–217.

Peterson, J. (2021). Family or Career? *Tweet.* Retrieved September 22, 2021, from http://twitter.com/jordanbpeterson/status/1440424855384453120

Proser, J. (2020). *Savage Messiah: How Dr. Jordan Peterson is saving Western civilization.* St Martin's Press

Thompson, E. (1968) *The making of the English working class.* Penguin Books, p9.

Winlow, S., Hall, S., & Treadwell, J. (2017). *The rise of the right: English nationalism and the transformation of working-class politics.* Polity Press

Xu, X., & Peterson, J. (2017). Differences in media preference mediate the link between personality and political orientation. *Political Psychology, 38*(1), 55–72.

---

[9] As Proser (2020) notes this argument about the role of YouTube in the configuration of Jordan Peterson's 'fame'.

[10] Disintermediated media are particularly important to the Jordan Peterson story. Because he was able to communicate directly with 'followers' on YouTube, Twitter and Facebook, and critiques of his views deployed the same platforms, very different interpretations emerged. Helen Lewis stated that, "people were consuming completely different Petersons, dependent on their news sources," from Lewis (2021).

[11] Brabazon (2014).

Chapter 4
Rule 3–Laugh like a Medusa and maintain the confidence of a mediocre white man

Laughter is powerful. It rebukes. It ridicules. It frightens. It creates a community. It recalibrates power relationships, even temporarily. I have often wondered if critics had laughed at Margaret Thatcher, Ronald Reagan or Scott Morrison, rather than take the often-ludicrous performance of power seriously, would the world have been different? The commitment to the market, the individual, and a particular rendering of masculinity, femininity and families has presented a disturbing bill to the world. Laughter makes trouble and creates instability.

The stunning nature of Jordan Peterson's public lectures is how bland, banal and boring they are. When the Peterson fame bubble started to emerge in 2016, I was expecting a powerful speaker, an EP Thompson, a Stuart Hall, a Maya Angelou. Instead, we watched a bland, mediocre scholar cite the bible, Solzhenitsyn, Jung and Dostoyevsky. Repeatedly. The lack of laughter—the pseudo religious worship - for the mediocre and predictable presentations tells us a lot about our time. For a writer so fixated on men and masculinity, Jordon Peterson has a high-pitched voice, thin and lithe body, and hand gestures that could inspire a Dusty Springfield drag queen. Therefore, when Jordan Peterson asked Camille Paglia for advice about feminism or postmodernism,[1] it was like asking a white pointer shark about vegetarianism.

That metaphor operates on many levels.

Paglia and Peterson valued the separate spheres—men in one sphere—women in another. The binaries are edifices blocking light and diversity and alternatives. The destiny of women is not and must never be determined by what goes in or comes out of vaginas. And speaking of vaginas, we need to talk about Donald Trump and his pussy grabbing.[2] The laughter that greeted the Presidency of Donald Trump was effective in delivering his fate as a one-term president. In his first year, *The President's Show*,

---

[1] Peterson (2017) .

[2] I note Greene (2021). He stated that, "ask most men, regardless of where they are on the political spectrum and they'll tell you. Something feels off. Something is not right," p. 12.

was a magnificent intervention—through grotesque excess—of what the programme described as, "the 45th and last president of the United States."[3] Laughter erupted in response to Donald Trump's speech at the United Nations.[4] Then—of course—there is the legendary Sarah Cooper, using the Covid lockdown to learn how to use TikTok, inventing a mode of miming and ventriloquy where the puppet suddenly gains control of the puppeteer.[5] The capacity to use President Trump's actual words, with sound cut away from vision, and to re-perform these speeches as a woman, will remain amongst the funniest moments of the pandemic-punctuated 2020. A woman, in a domestic environment, on a playful and marginalized platform, undermined the president more than any *New York Times* article. Why was this method so effective? In tough times, Sarah Cooper recognized the blistering and angry power of laughter. When women laugh, it is transgressive and builds a community. That is why women's laughter has been feared. Men fear women's laughter. They should. Sometimes it is undermined through clichés such as 'giggling like a schoolgirl,' but the raucous, snorting laughter from a group of women cannot be beaten for shrivelling and pricking the pomposity of men.

When women laugh together, we share something. Patriarchy works to separate women: gay and straight, trans and cis, races, religions, ages and classes. Laughter is rebellion, and when we share laughter, we share literacy and context. Mikhail Bakhtin studied this mode of liberation through his history and theory of the carnival.[6] This temporary liberation flipped hierarchies and mocked religious morality. It is provocatively important in secular times, to think about how much we take seriously that should actually be sliced with laughter. Bakhtin showed that these carnivals in the Middle Ages were attacked by the church and the state so that by the seventeenth century they were banned. That is the disruptive power of inversion, mockery and laughter. Jo Anna Isaak showed that even when the carnival's power was destroyed, it continued to emerge in all-woman gatherings, such as the bedside of women who had given birth.[7] These communities of shared laughter were continued by women. They created space for bodies, for difference, and embodied alternatives outside of religion and sin. Bakhtin confirmed that these events were, "marked by abundant food and frank conversation."[8] The laughing woman holds power. Laughter is embodied critique and the occupation of space with laughter cannot be patrolled by ridiculing phrases like, "What are you laughing at?" and "What's so funny?".

Laughter ruptures the tight framing of women, trapped between genitalia and brain, silence and shame, visible and invisible, passive and active, and compliant and competing. Instead of women recovering and reclaiming, what if we re-language the feminist goal to confounding and cackling. Women have minimized the scale of our potential when we attempt to rebuild—and reclaim—the relationship between

---

[3] The President's Show, Comedy Central, 2017.

[4] Trump (2018).

[5] Sarah Cooper Comedy, https://www.youtube.com/channel/UCySwUJIFN_tECtGX3xbjAGQ.

[6] Bakhtin (1941).

[7] Isaak (1997).

[8] Bakhtin, *op. cit.*, p. 50.

femininity and competence.[9] We set our standards of behaviour too low. It is time to summon the commitment of Gloria Gaynor, the courage of Lady Gaga (and her wardrobe), the sass of Beyonce and the intensity of Joni Mitchell. Women's narratives can take many directions. With courage, we can transcend the mantras of women's leadership style,[10] and occupy space in our plurality and diversity.

Jordan Peterson is a bloke in a suit. He is given gravitas because he is in a suit. He is not funny. Even his jokes are not funny. Yet he summons a feminism in his speeches and writing—which is unrecognizable to feminists - that patrols fun and pleasure. Supposedly, we feminists stop men having a good time. Actually, I am not hugely interested in how men occupy time, good or otherwise. Instead, my focus is women and I welcome transgressive and transformative dialogues with trans colleagues and non-binary identifying citizens. We learn from the brutality of the debates encircling TERFs that careful and respectful work is required to build new communities and configure new intellectual and social partnerships. I am intent on returning the Laughing Medusa to the toolkit of contemporary feminism. Jordan Peterson was somewhat fixated on Foucault, Lacan and Derrida. He found them difficult, and there was no evidence through citation or analysis that he read them. Indeed, for Peterson, Foucault is played by Derrida.[11] Althusser is played by identity politics. Jordan Peterson configured himself as the hero in a very unfunny zombie apocalypse movie.

Significantly, Peterson neglected the frighteningly remarkable work of the feminist poststructuralists. It is time to acknowledge the heritage of Helene Cixous. Her essay—"The Laugh of the Medusa"—changed my life.[12] I do not know if I would have become a writer without this essay. I read it at 21 and it is probably the most motivational prose about a woman writing in the history of feminist non-fiction, even acknowledging the riveting splendour of Virginia Woolf's *A room of one's own*.[13] "The Laugh of the Medusa" was published in 1976. Distanced from the white heat of the second wave, we forget Cixous's power.

> I shall speak about women's writing: about what we will do. Woman must write her self: must write about women and bring women to writing, from which they have been driven away as violently as from their bodies. Woman must put herself into the text—as into the world and into history—by her own movement.[14]

> Women must write through their bodies, they must submerge, cut through, get beyond the ultimate reverse-discourse, including the one that laughs at the very idea of pronouncing the

---

[9] While critiquing this position, I log the powerful work of Kaseman (1998).

[10] Jewell and Whicker (1993).

[11] This is a fascinating inversion, and ironic considering that both Derrida and Peterson are post-Heideggerian. Peterson continually configured Derrida as a nihilist. That is incorrect. Derrida confirmed that it was possible for logocentrism to be transcended.

[12] Cixous (1976).

[13] Woolf (1929).

[14] Cixous, *op. cit.*, p. 875.

word 'silence.' You only have to look at the Medusa straight on to see her. And she's not deadly. She's beautiful and she's laughing.[15]

The lesson from Cixous is do not be well adjusted. Occupy space. Occupy silence. Make trouble. At this point in our history, one way we as women make trouble is to call out injustices through our laughter. Sarah Hagi's great slogan—"Lord, grant me the confidence of a mediocre white man"[16]—captures this imperative.

Redistribution of wealth is a major issue. So is the redistribution of confidence. Ponder the men who apply for promotion within a year of starting a new job and the women who wait a decade. The blokes that ask for a pay increase while colleagues are made redundant. The men who speak and speak and speak—like Jordan Peterson about the bible, Solzhenitsyn, Dostoyevsky and Jung—without reading these authors or beyond them, or the women who apologise for offering a view on the basis of their career of research. Or worse. The women who sit in silence, disenfranchised from sound and space. What if a generation of women stopped apologizing for living in the world? What if women could ask for what they want? What if women expressed their ideas and were not wedded to how they are received? What if women made themselves the stars of their own lives? What if women learned from other women and supported them on their journey? What if women activated strategic binarism to transcend social, cultural and theoretical binaries imposed on them by the Alt-Right and build new partnerships and dialogues?

Men's confidence is a gift. It comes from moving through the world and the world not hitting back too hard, too often. It comes from recognizing that wearing a polyester suit loans expertise and gravitas to the wearer. When women claim space and voice, and gain support from other women, changes jut into our culture. The pompous must trigger laughter not fear. Hollow arguments summon giggles and guffaws and—most importantly - writing back to the shallow, the shambling, the pretentious and the banal.

References

Bakhtin, M. (1941). *Rabelais and his world*. Indiana University Press
Cooper, S. Comedy. *YouTube Channel*. https://www.youtube.com/channel/UCySwUJIFN_tECt GX3xbjAGQ
Cixous, H. (1976). The laugh of the medusa. *Signs, 1*, 875–93.
Greene, M. (2021). *Remaking manhood in the age of Trump*. ThinkPlay Partners
Hagi, S., & Shaw, R. (2016). Grant every woman the confidence of a mediocre white man. *Ideas at the House*. https://medium.com/all-about-women/grant-every-woman-the-confidence-of-a-med iocre-white-man-e6f9b9d0cc5f
Isaak, J. (1997). *Laughter ten years after*. University of British Columbia. https://belkin.ubc.ca/exh ibitions/laughter-ten-years-after/

---

[15] ibid., p. 893.

[16] Hagi and Shaw (2016). Please note: the original statement came from Sarah Hagi's Twitter account, which has subsequently closed.

Jewell, M., & Whicker, M. (1993). The feminization of leadership in state legislatures. *PS: Political Science and Politics, 26*(4).

Kaseman, D. (1998). Beyond the double bind: Women and leadership. *Women and Language, 21*(2), 49–55.

Peterson, J., Paglia, C. (2017). Modern times with Camille Paglia and Jordan Peterson. *YouTube.* October 3, 2017. https://www.youtube.com/watch?v=v-hIVnmUdXM

Trump, D. (2018). President Donald Trump gets unexpected laugh at United Nations. *BBC News.* September 26, 2018. https://www.youtube.com/watch?v=eN2jqTilLOM

Woolf, V. (1929). *A room of one's own.* Harcourt, Brace and Company

Chapter 5
Rule 4–Empowered groups have to be confident in their power to give some away

The political right and left are filled with brittle masculinities, lashing out at women, cutting away their power, collaborations and conversation. Jordan Peterson is on the stranger end of these personal struggles. To reference his first book, *Maps of Meaning*:

> I came home late one night from a college drinking party, self-disgusted and angry. I took a canvas board and some paints. I sketched a harsh, crude picture of a crucified Christ–glaring and demonic–with a cobra wrapped around his naked waist, like a belt.[1]

There is so much happening in this statement. The complexity and oddity mask a simple truth. Heterosexual, white men maintain the identity politics that dares not speak its name. Instead, the masks that cover this truth are dangerous. As Peterson worryingly confirmed, "I dreamed apocalyptic dreams."[2] He described his project as "to make sense of the human capacity, my capacity, for evil—particularly for those evils associated with belief."[3] These are dark thoughts. Of greater concern is that these darker thoughts are being shared as self help with and for young men.[4] A tip for punters: the moment any of us are inspired to paint a deity with reptilian accoutrements, it is time to lay off the tequila.

Christopher Hitchens, famously if ambivalently positioned on the left through much of his life, was similarly confused at the empowered feminine—but thankfully without painting Christ with a cobra belt. In *Hitch 22*, women were described as

---

[1] Peterson (1999).

[2] ibid., xviii.

[3] ibid., xix.

[4] The period of Jordan Peterson's profile also saw the rise of the Incels, the 'Involuntary celibate.' These are the men who—supposedly—are not selected by women for sex and respond with bitterness, anger and violence. This community directs their animosity to 'Stacys,' the objectified women they cannot attract, and the 'Chads' who obtain the most attractive partners and dominate the sexual 'marketplace.' I acknowledge the strong research by Brian Van Brunt and Chris Taylor in the investigation of this 'community' (2021).

T. Brabazon, *12 Rules for (Academic) Life*,
https://doi.org/10.1007/978-981-16-9291-8_5

having a "magically beautiful face,"[5] or "cynical little witches,"[6] "bitch,"[7] "feisty,"[8] "Hitch-proof,"[9] "haggard,"[10] "tempestuous,"[11] "glamorous"[12] or—on multiple occasions—the wife of someone important. Although I rarely use the phrase 'white privilege' because it is a blunt and ill-aimed intellectual instrument, it was justified in clear and stark terms when reviewing this book.

> we earned our claim to speak and intervene by right of experience and sacrifice and work. It would never have done for any of us to stand up and say that our sex or sexuality or pigmentation or disability were qualifications in themselves.[13]

Straw women, straw sexuality, straw race and straw disability are assembled in a tidy row in *Hitch 22* to justify marginalization and irrelevance. If able-bodied white men are not the centre of the conversation, then any other success has been achieved through the lowering of standards or qualifications. Let that sentence marinate for a moment. For Hitchens, if a woman or a person of colour or a person with a disability gains success, profile or financial security, then 'the system' has been gerrymandered to skew and reduce the requirements and responsibilities demanded of men to reach the same level of achievement. This is one explanation/justification for the downward mobility of white men. It can be blamed on 'freeloading migrants' or 'welfare mothers.' There are other reasons why white men are confronting failure or under-achievement, by Hitch's standards. Clearly though, under-employed men with time on their hands, angry and self-absorbed, do not question the extreme profit margins of corporations and the global movement of capital. It is much easier to troll tweet a feminist who appeared on morning television.[14]

Jordan Peterson maintains—extraordinarily—the Hitchens melody. When noting the life narratives of such men, similarities may seem stark and peculiar. They are worth noting. For both, the focus is to critique identity politics. Scholars from many backgrounds, paradigms and political inflections have implemented this critique. But the key difference in the case of Hitchens and Peterson is they use this critique to justify the power held by white men. Any questioning of this power is slopped into the bucket of identity politics. Indeed, Jordan Peterson wrote and recorded a

---

[5] Hitchens (2010).

[6] ibid., p. 82.

[7] ibid., p. 82.

[8] ibid., p. 115.

[9] ibid., p. 108.

[10] ibid, p. 32.

[11] ibid., p. 267.

[12] ibid., p. 44.

[13] ibid., p. 63.

[14] Whitney Phillips stated that "not only do trolls scavenge, repurpose, and weaponize myriad aspects of mainstream culture (all the better to troll you with), mainstream culture normalizes and at times actively celebrates precisely those attitudes and behaviors that in trolling contexts are said to be aberrant, antisocial, and cruel," from *This is why we can't have nice things: mapping the relationship between online trolling and mainstream culture*, (Cambridge: MIT Press, 2015), p. 49.

long lecture titled, "Identity politics and the Marxist lie of white privilege."[15] Such narratives are the story arc of masculinity for young white men. These men—right and left—offer pathways that seem clear, logical and rational. They offer a directive for young men away from chaos, which is defined by the capacity to negotiate, think about alternatives, and question whether one version of experience, sacrifice and work is any better or greater than those who have taken a different path. Zizek is not excluded from this critique. In a 2016 article he stated,

> The true danger comes with the reasoning that only a lesbian single mother can understand what it means to be a lesbian single mother, or that only a gay man can understand what it means to be gay. I think such a view, such an undermining of universality, is catastrophic.[16]

For such an intelligent man, Zizek has also fallen into the easy argument that straight white men are the universal truth, and every other group does not possess a view of value, knowledge, experience or expertise that is meaningful. He has form for such missteps. He has asked—and not rhetorically—"Do men simply earn more because they are more competent?"[17] Men earn more than women, because women dominate health and education industries, which in a STEM-ified age are not as valued as much as engineering or corporate management. Men earn more than women because women shoulder the overwhelming majority of household duties and tasks. Men earn more than women because women assume the bulk of caring responsibilities for children and elderly parents. Men earn more than women because women are seen as women, rather than workers, engineers, health care professionals or doctors. Women are more than ovaries. Indeed, women may not have ovaries. Instead of recognizing the knowledge systems beyond himself, Hitchens, Peterson and Zizek (quite a combination) use identity politics as an excuse to explain why women will not play well with others, politically, intellectually or socially. Intriguingly the far left and the far right both critique 'identity politics,' yet the meaning of this phrase remains volatile and obscured.

What Zizek confirms through this selection of a "lesbian single mother" as an example in his argument is that identity politics is located as far away as possible from the heterosexual procreative man. Heterosexual men do not have identity politics. They just have an identity. And politics. But when housed in the body of a heterosexual man, the words 'identity' and 'politics' are sheafed by other terms: humans, citizens, writers, scholars or workers. Straight men do not have politics. They have life, reality and truth. Any other social formation only performs identity politics, because those citizens cannot get over themselves to engage with (you are ahead of me, dear reader) life, reality and truth. Put another way, and citing Albert Einstein, always known for the pithy quotation:

---

[15] Peterson (2017).
[16] Zizek (2016).
[17] Zizek (2020).

If my theory of relativity is proven correct, Germany will claim me as a German and France will declare that I am a citizen of the world. Should my theory prove untrue, France will say that I am a German and Germany will declare that I am a Jew.[18]

Women understand this differentiation. If we are not quite good enough, we are a woman in STEM or a feminist scholar. If we have made it, then we are an historian, a physicist, or an archaeologist.

Zizek has also let the Alt-Right off the hook. There have been many errors and flaws in critiquing the Alt-Right. The attention and focus must remain on what Nicholas Michelsen and Pablo De Orellana described as "the politics of resisting modernity."[19] What is clear is when evangelical Christianity aligns with corporate interests, modernity becomes one more blockage in the manosphere, alongside feminazis and terrorists. Therefore women, citizens of colour, migrants, non-binary identifying people, trans communities—our identity shopping list can continue—must speak their truth, claim their experience, sacrifice and work, share their knowledge, and claim plurality. This is political ping pong. The Alt-Right need identity politics, and identity politics activists require the Alt-Right. But the only available alternative is in refusal: to not to sit in the singularity of white men, assuming universality and generalizability. This inelegant and reified mode of generalization no longer operates effectively as a social or political strategy. It never did. As Andrew Manno confirmed, "following the rules of traditional masculinity doesn't fit with a modern workplace that generally requires constant communication, cooperation, and collaboration."[20] Effort and intentionality are required to build the connections, relationships, affinities and communication systems, to activate power through diversity. Sitting in the self may provide comfort and confidence. With a data set of one—the self—it is satisfying to perpetuate importance, value, intelligence and competence. Stretching and transcending our lived identity through reading, writing and researching history is the foundation for social change. One person holds rights. That is important. However, through research, explanations can emerge as to how those 'rights' were created and why they matter. This is even more urgent and important.

References

Hitchens, C. (2010). *Hitch 22* (p. 122). Hatchette Press.
Manno, A. (2020). *Toxic masculinity, casino capitalism, and America's favorite card game: The poker mindset* (p. 31). Springer.

---

[18] The original citation for this reference is believed to have appeared in the *New York Times* in early 1930. Like most Einstein maxims, the original citation is difficult to determine. In this case, it appeared to have emerged in a lecture at the Sorbonne in 1929, and then printed the following year in the *New York Times*. A reference is confirmed in *Good Reads*, 2021, https://www.goodreads.com/quotes/93643-if-my-theory-of-relativity-is-proven-successful-germany-will.

[19] Michelsen and De Orellana (2019).

[20] Manno (2020).

Michelsen, N., & De Orellana, P. (2019). Discourses of resilience in the US Alt-Right. *Resilience, 7*(3), 275.

Peterson, J. (1999). *Maps of meaning* (p. xix). Routledge.

Peterson, J. (2017). Identity politics and the Marxist lie of white privilege. YouTube, November 14, 2017, Identity politics and the Marxist lie of white privilege – YouTube.

Van Brunt, B. & Taylor, C. (2021). *Understanding and treating Incels: case studies, guidance, and treatment of violence risk in the involuntary celibate community*, New York: Routledge.

Zizek, S. (2016, 26 May). Migrants, racists and the left. *Spiked*.

Zizek, S. (2020). Jordan Peterson as a symptom of … What? In B. Burgis, C. Hamilton, M. McManus, & M. Trejo (Eds.), *Myth and Mayhem: a leftist critique of Jordan Peterson*, p. 12. Winchester: Zero Books.

Chapter 6
Rule 5–Intellectual generosity is the foundation of scholarly life

So much of academic life is filled with trivialities, jealousy and envy. Scholars can bully and undermine.[1] Ignore or gaslight. This context summons a selfishness and self-absorption that freezes ideas, people and life around them. Academics label, gossip, block and attack, rather than care, respect and enable.

It is easy to blame and displace. But this Rule and commentary is not about other people. Greetings, dear reader. This is the audience participation moment of this book. Think about how you feel and react when a colleague produces new research. Do you congratulate them, read it, share it, comment on Facebook or Twitter, and cite it? Conversely, do resentment and jealousy bubble in your throat with the attendant soundtrack of Vicki Lawrence's "It could have been me"?[2]

Being a scholar is tough, particularly in anti-intellectual times. Make no mistake and offer no platitudes about the nature of our context. We are clearly and profoundly in anti-intellectual times. This is an era where expertise is denied, and experience is its sloppy replacement. Commentators sprout with great confidence about what is wrong with schools and universities. If a person attended school, then they can talk about schooling, teaching, learning and teachers. Obviously. They have a data point of one. They attended school. Further, people who have graduated from an undergraduate degree at university, or - in the case of 'journalists' on the right like Andrew Bolt - did not finish an undergraduate degree at university,[3] suddenly gain the confidence of Johnny Rotten at the Roxy in 1976. Scholars can complain about this disrespect, or we can do something. It is appropriate and necessary to summon scholarly debates. Ideas are important. Reading divergent views is crucial to the development of research. Reading, writing, thinking, interpreting and analysing are the building blocks for the creation of knowledge.

This is the problem with Jordan Peterson. It is not that he references the bible. Well, not really. It is not the inability to cite women academics. It is not even the

---

[1] Lester (2013).

[2] Lawrence, "It could have been me," *YouTube*, https://youtu.be/WQ1bOjevvGY.

[3] Andrew Bolt (2021).

© The Author(s), under exclusive license to Springer Nature Singapore Pte Ltd. 2022   37
T. Brabazon, *12 Rules for (Academic) Life*,
https://doi.org/10.1007/978-981-16-9291-8_6

meat diet.[4] Do you want more meat with your meat? The problem is a lack of reading. Peterson runs a small clinical psychology practice. He lectured about big ideas detailing 'the human condition' in a course he ran for over a decade. Whenever I read, watch or listen to Jordan Peterson, I summon the great maxim from the late—and great—Tony Wilson: "If you get it, great. If you don't, that's fine too. But you should probably read more."[5] The point is, Peterson has not read the ideas that he is disagreeing with, as the Zizek debate demonstrated in excruciating fashion. An intellectual supports scholars by reading their work. We can disagree. That is productive and important. But intellectual generosity is demonstrated by taking the time and infusing research with the scholarship of others. Social media allow and encourage comment and communication, to be part of a community. Digital media are deterritorialized and disintermediated. That means that feminist scholarship can move outside of gatekeepers. But this diversity also presents risks, as information obesity can emerge.[6] Scholars require digital dieting and information literacy to find, assess and value the calibre of research. Some scholars may see social media as self-promotion and, particularly if women academics are not supported in their institution, confidence can be lacking in the considered deployment of Twitter, YouTube or Instagram for enabling research dissemination.

There remains value in entering public discourse in different ways. Consider Brexit. Ponder the Trump presidency. Evaluate the often mediocre and frequently bizarre decision making that undergirds the construction of public policy. In such a time, researchers are valuable because we engage with and commit to ideas, evidence and argument. The taxpayers—the citizens who pay the wages of university academics—have a right to find and read high quality information, rather than gibberish. Using open access academic journals and a media strategy, we as scholars are enabling a citizenship where xenophobia, ignorance and fear are critiqued. This is positive. This is powerful. It is a reminder that each of us are scholars in the world, and for the world. Citizens can read our research or ignore it, attack it or ridicule it, but the presence of refereed scholarship increases the rights and choices of people to consider evidence, interpret ideas and engage with the theories of others. If this commitment is not enacted, then vulgar and inelegant journalism will be returned in Google searches. For example, *The Australian* newspaper columnist Greg Sheridan, blamed "the Left" and "postmodernism" for the terror attack on the Al Noor Mosque in Christchurch in 2019.

> Two modern ideologies do find echoes in the Christchurch manifesto. One is identity politics. The only value the manifesto positively asserts is race. It is the Left that is making race and identity the centre of all politics ... Finally, the postmodern view that there is no objective truth, that, as Michel Foucault put it, the 'regime of truth,' rationality itself, is oppressive, allows everybody, not just people like you, to construct their own fantasy reality. As Christchurch demonstrates, those fantasies can be nightmares.[7]

---

[4] Hamblin (2018).

[5] Wilson, "Icarus," Quote Tab, https://www.quotetab.com/quote/by-tony-wilson/ill-just-say-one-word-icarus-if-you-get-it-great-if-you-dont-thats-fine-t#k0fZL7VM0KiT2wyS.97.

[6] Brabazon (2013).

[7] Sheridan (2019).

For those who may have either forgotten the facts of this case or had their mind furniture moved by the noise expressed by Sheridan, the Christchurch terrorist attack at the Al Noor Mosque and the Linwood Islamic Centre during Friday prayer was enacted by a lone gunman. He killed 51 people and injured 40 people. These brutalizing murders were conducted by Brenton Harrison Terrant, a white Australian, from Grafton in New South Wales. Research into his background confirmed he was not only a white supremacist, but part of the Alt-Right. To add further poison to this murderous brew, he livestreamed the shooting on Facebook. What is the relevance of "the postmodern view" to the understanding of this act of stunning inhumanity? The answer is—obviously—that this theoretical perspective from three decades in the past has no role, function, place or purpose in this narrative. It is a lens. A distraction. A patsy. There is, however, a more important issue here. This is the level of 'interpretation' offered by a journalist in a national newspaper. This is not on TikTok. This is not an 'influencer' on Instagram. This is a journalist from a national newspaper. Therefore, it is crucial that academics summon our intellectual role, to counter, critique and reveal this excuse for an argument. Mentioning two ideas—the killing of 51 people in a Mosque and postmodernism—in the same paragraph does not mean they are linked. Indeed, they are not. But we learn a great deal about the state of journalism through the forceful adhering of two ideas that have no affiliation except to excuse a white Australian man who killed other humans with a different faith structure or perhaps skin colour.

Scholars can allow Jordan Peterson to continue to release banality, or we can—with intellectual courage—share our work so that others can learn from it. Intellectual generosity emerges when reading and engaging with the research of others, not with jealousy, not with rudeness, but in the context of a safe and robust engagement with ideas. The mechanism for a thinking readership is:

Open access.

Decency.

Integrity.

Respect for intelligence.

Respect for qualifications.

Respect for ideas.

When combined, these attributes summon leadership. I am aware we live in cruel times where knowledge is corporatized, and citizens are exploited and discarded like junk thrown into landfill. But we—today—can make a decision to show some dignity, and respect the intelligent while also respecting diversity and ideas. Each of us have lived a distinctive life story, with different goals. Higher education must never be Fordist, pumping out graduates to subsidize industries with little respect for learning or professional development. Higher education must be bespoke and customized. Corporate education is offered as an alternative, with Jordan Peterson's company, Luminate Enterprises, "working on an app that helps university students write essays."[8] This was reported by his daughter, the CEO of his company. Her educational qualifications include a period at Concordia University, reading psychology

---

[8] Peterson (2021).

and classics between 2011 and 2013. She moved to George Brown Continuing Education College between 2013 and 2014 with a specialism in makeup. She then enrolled at Ryerson University to gain a Bachelor of Biological and Biomedical Sciences, between 2014 and 2016.[9] Jordan Peterson holds Bachelor degrees in political science and psychology from the University of Alberta and a PhD in clinical psychology from McGill University.[10] The key absence to recognize in this presentation of qualifications is that no education, teaching or learning expertise has been gained through their academic histories. So, this 'app' is being developed to help students write essays. Yet the father and daughter team leading this company have no educational qualifications. This—indeed—is a story of and from our time.

Intellectual generosity is investing in service, not individual ego at the cost of colleagues and knowledge, and reading with quiet reflection, deep listening about needs, wishes and goals, and lifting the quality of research to enable citizenship. Teaching and learning are radical acts. They provide hope through despair. This hope, no matter the scale of the countervailing evidence in the present, is activated by the possibilities of a better future. In building this connection between critique and celebration, fixity and possibilities, present and future, universities serve our society. This service is not to placate the mediocre and the acquiescing, but to question the easy stories and narratives we have been hearing all our lives, and to enliven standards without standardization.

The model of intellectual generosity for me—perhaps not surprisingly considering the state of our universities at the moment—emerged outside of higher education. Indeed, it jutted from popular culture. I want our universities to be like the final forty seconds of the 2006 *Canadian Songwriters Hall of Fame*.[11] KD Lang sings the Leonard Cohen song "Hallelujah." Let us consider this scene. An old 1960s 'radical,' heterosexual man, poet turned pop star, skated between popular and unpopular culture throughout his career. He was being honoured in his home country by fellow Canadian KD Lang, a proud and politicized lesbian, who is in possession of one of the greatest singing voices in the world. But Lang's remarkable performance is not the model of the future university I want to summon. What occurs at the conclusion of the performance is meaningful. Lang—while acknowledging a standing ovation for one of the best live performances in the history of recorded popular music—stepped off the stage and bowed her head as she approached Cohen in the front row. She greeted him with a namaste, which at its most basic translation is 'the god in me acknowledges the god in you.' She continued to bow her head and Cohen allowed her this acknowledgement. But then he looked her in the eyes, touched both her hands, and kissed them. She then returned to the stage and he to his seat. Two very different people. Different histories. Different talents. But they met, acknowledged

---

[9] These were the qualifications confirmed on Mikhaila Peterson's LinkedIn profile and repeated through other sites. Please refer to Mikhaila Peterson, *LinkedIn*, https://www.linkedin.com/in/mikhailapeterson/?originalSubdomain=ca.

[10] "Jordan Peterson," *Linkedin*, https://www.linkedin.com/in/jordanbpeterson/?originalSubdomain=ca.

[11] Leonard Cohen and K.D. Lang Hallelujah (2006).

their differences, acknowledged their abilities, and acknowledged their connection. That is intellectual generosity.

References

Andrew Bolt. (2021). *Desmog.* https://www.desmogblog.com/andrew-bolt,

Brabazon, T. (2013). *Digital Dieting: From information obesity to intellectual fitness.* Ashgate.

Hamblin, J. (2018, 28 August). The Jordan Peterson all meat diet. The Atlantic. https://www.theatl antic.com/health/archive/2018/08/the-peterson-family-meat-cleanse/567613/.

Lester, J. (2013). *Workplace bullying in higher education.* Routledge.

Cohen, L. and Lang, K.D. (2006). Hallelujah. Canadian Songwriters Hall of Fame. *YouTube.* https://www.youtube.com/watch?v=YYiMJ2bC65A.

Peterson, M. (2021, 1 March). How we built the Jordan Peterson media empire. *National Post.* https://nationalpost.com/news/canada/mikhaila-peterson-how-we-built-the-jor dan-peterson-media-empire.

Sheridan, G. (2019, 23 March). A manifesto for a dark age. *The Australian*, p. 20.

Chapter 7
Rule 6–Simply because you work in a university does not mean you are an expert in higher education

I have never understood why a PhD is the gateway qualification into an academic career. It is an apprenticeship for research but the idea that a PhD offers any capacity to prepare academics to write curriculum and teach or to contribute to public debates is bizarre. A PhD is an original contribution to knowledge in a particular field. Refereed scholarship is verified by gatekeepers in scholarly journals. Research that is verified and reviewed is important and valuable. Yet the complete lack of expertise in teaching and learning and professional writing means that the only tool kit academics possess is homology. They repeat what they were taught—and teach it to others. This process is conservative, validates nostalgia, and creates an imagined past that does not exist. As Peterson infers, "those who tend toward the right, politically, are staunch defenders of all that has worked in the past. And much of the time, they are correct in being so."[1] This is an archetypal Peterson argument. He is accurate that—before the arrival of the Alt-Right, conservatives maintained and valued the status quo. Progressives agitated for change. But his second sentence is not only ideological and argumentative, it is the equivalent of pouring cheap barbeque sauce over elegantly sauteed salmon. The past remains a foreign country.[2] It is unknowable in its complexity and diversity. This argument holds for an understanding of our universities. The history of universities is inspiring and powerful. It has also been exclusionary and inhibiting of social change. Both these arguments may be accurate and validated through evidence. But we learn about how Peterson engages with higher education through the mode of argument summoned in these two sentences.

Simply because we have the privilege of working in a university does not mean we are an expert in higher education studies. Simply because we drink milk does not mean we are an expert in dairy farming. This confusion of experience and expertise is a problem and challenge, which is why it is important to keep completing qualifications, continuing to read, continuing to challenge ourselves with inter, trans, post and multidisciplinary knowledge. Jordan Peterson is perhaps the most astonishing

---

[1] Peterson (2021).

[2] Hartley (1958).

T. Brabazon, *12 Rules for (Academic) Life*,
https://doi.org/10.1007/978-981-16-9291-8_7

example of a scholar who takes a very narrow expertise (clinical psychology), has only worked in a few elite institutions, and yet tries to assemble a worldview about higher education. When a moment emerged that required a reconfiguration and recalibration of student identities in his classroom, he did not have the resources to manage it.[3] Beyond the trans community, his ignorance of wider higher educational issues is revealed in his commentary on the humanities and the arts. His critique of disciplines with intellectual legacies from the foundations of university history is nasty, ignorant and bundled into a wider ignorance of STEM, men, women and politics.

> Men are bailing out of the humanities like mad and pretty much out of the universities, except for STEM. The women are moving in like mad, and they're also moving into the political sphere like mad. This is new. We've never had this happen before, and we do not know what the significance of it is. It's only 50 years old.[4]

It is uncertain what—precisely—is only 50 years old. Elizabeth I—or Elizabeth II—seems to counter his 50-year rule for politics. Women have been part of our universities for centuries, fighting for the right to graduate with a degree. Intriguingly, the exclusions of women from universities were not his focus or interest. It is the movement of men—and the credibility and importance that they carry—that is significant. This is the change he finds unsettling. Men are not graduating from universities at a higher rate than women. This disparity, based on hard work, achievement, assessment and repetitive testing at earlier educational levels, is supposedly a problem. Women in education and politics are—seemingly—a concern. Why? What is so important about ovaries and breasts that they discharge the capacity to read, think, interpret and lead? What is so important about a penis and scrotum that summons a disposition and gift for public policy or research? Yes, I will state the obvious. The repetitive use of 'like mad' captures—for Peterson—the irrationality of change, of women gaining education and power. Once more, those operating outside of these distinct gendered and sexualized divisions are invisible within this debate.

Jordan Peterson is not an expert in higher education studies. He holds bachelor degrees in psychology and political science and a PhD in clinical psychology. He holds no educational qualification. Further, he discusses STEM without any qualifications in physics, chemistry, mathematics, biology, computer science or environmental science. He discusses the humanities without any qualifications in languages, philosophy, art and design, history, communication and media studies. His degrees and publications are in the applied social sciences. Why this clarity matters in the presentation of his expertise is that the hypocrisy and inconsistency of his arguments were made clear in *Beyond Order: 12 More Rules for Life*. He stated, "it is better to presume ignorance and invite learning than to assume sufficient knowledge and risk the consequent blindness."[5] Once more, he does not follow his own advice.

---

[3] I am reminded of Mary Trump's commentary about her uncle: "Donald has, in some sense, always been institutionalized, shielded from his limitations," from *Too much and never enough: how my family created the world's most dangerous man*, (London: Simon and Schuster, 2020), p. 15.

[4] Peterson (2019).

[5] Peterson (2021).

Through the publication of his second self-help book that only intensified the banality and contradictions, Jordan Peterson's story became increasingly odd. An outlier. An outsider. I use 'outsider' as configured by Steve Richards.

> The outsiders are varied, but in an era of vague slogans and assertions they are easily defined. Some are from the right and some from the left, but they come from outside orthodox mainstream democratic politics. A lot of them are not elected to their national parliament.[6]

Richards makes the point that outsiders emerge because leaders, political parties, journalists and academics—to name a few institutions and occupations—did not spend the time to configure an argument that was convincing to the majority of the population. Assertions too easily spilled into truths. Therefore, it is no surprise that outsiders deployed the same strategies, offering often odd opinions and verifying them through the force of a personality rather than the persuasion of an argument with evidence. Why Peterson is unusual in occupying outsider status is that he is an academic. We, as scholars, read, test, analyse, interpret and verify. Our arguments are scaffolded by references. We configure an argument one footnote at a time, and leave the footnotes public and visible for our analysis to be checked. Yet from such an occupation, Peterson has become an outsider. What makes this identification even more peculiar is that Peterson has lived a conventional academic career. In 1998 he was appointed a full professor at the University of Toronto, while maintaining a clinical practice. He was a good lecturer. Some solid citations emerged for co-authored work, as is the norm in clinical psychology. Significantly, he is rarely the first or last author, occupying the position often described as the "freeloading postdoc" role. This traditional professional life was mirrored in his private life. He married a woman he met during his childhood, and had two children. This is all very conventional.

Something happened in the mid-2010s. Perhaps in a desire for public acclaim or profile, from 2013 he uploaded YouTube lectures[7] on religion[8] and self-help. These lectures were conservative in form and content, riffing off headings and prompts, rather than revealing detailed, complex knowledge. By September 2016, he posted the video on Canada's Bill C-16, an Act to Amend Canada's Human Rights Act and

---

[6] Richards (2017).

[7] The oddity of the videos themselves are worthy of attention. Many of his videos are lectures that have been recorded. Lectures—at their best—are geared for analogue, multi-sensory experiences. They are also teaching opportunities for very specific courses and learning outcomes. But Tabatha Southey offers an interpretation of these videos. She states, "Peterson's videos go on and on. It's like opening up a tab for one of those bird nest webcams at the height of its popularity: Lots of people are watching, you feel like you should too, but nothing is happening," from "Is Jordan Peterson the stupid man's smart person," *MacLean's*, November 17, 2017, Is Jordan Peterson the stupid man's smart person? - Macleans.ca.

[8] It is always important to note that, as Peterson stated about his background, "I attended conservative Protestant services during childhood with my mother," and "I was raised under the protective auspices, so to speak, of the Christian church," from J. Peterson (1999).

Criminal Code, from the liberal government of Justin Trudeau. It proposed that it was illegal for federal governments to discriminate against individuals on the basis of their gender expression. Attendant revisions were enacted in the Ontario Human Rights Code. Peterson read this change as censorship of speech and refused to comply to the demand that students be addressed by their preferred gender pronouns. He configured himself as a victim, that through this noncompliance, he could go to jail or lose his job. There was no chance of either. Indeed, in January 2022, he resigned from his tenured post at the University of Toronto. He accompanied this resignation with a dummy spit, quit lit article explaining that he was a victim of - you are ahead of me - political correctness. More worrying he stated that he could no longer teach because young men in his classroom had little chance of employment (Peterson 2022). Again, there is no evidence for his claims. He also did not differentiate between the Canadian Human Rights Act and the law that applies to his province, the Ontario Human Rights Code. Universities in Canada are regulated by the provincial code. This means he has been subjected to the legislation barring discrimination on gender identity in the workplace since 2012. Therefore, Jordan Peterson lacked the most basic, foundational information in making his case. Even though his facts were inaccurate and he was summoning a hollow victimhood, patrons donated to Peterson on Patreon and he gained a revenue stream that dwarfed his academic salary.[9] He suddenly became a free speech warrior and anti-trans activist.[10]

Then—through 2017 and 2018—the "Postmodern NeoMarxist"[11] gibberish emerged, and with it—overt attacks on what he describes as the radicalization of the university campus.[12] It was only in April 2019 during the public debate with Zizek that this public presentation confirmed that Peterson had no idea what he was talking about, no knowledge of Marxism, and little engagement with philosophy or philosophers. Actually, postmodernism and Marxism are most frequently antithetical. Postmodernism is a critique of Marxism and other master narratives. Indeed, some of the best-known theorists associated with postmodernism in some form, such as

---

[9] This donated income stream was reported as between $38,000 and $60,000 a month at the height of the 'compelled speech' debates. Please refer to J. Proser (2020).

[10] Similarly, the empowered people who questioned Jordan Peterson's right and ability to offer commentary on complex issues beyond his disciplinary expertise were also attacked and undermined. For example, when Vice Chancellor Stephen Toope resigned from Cambridge University, *The Spectator* described him as "the undistinguished Canadian lawyer" and blamed his failures on, "the humiliating treatment of Prof. Jordan Peterson, who had a non-paying fellowship withdrawn based on an equally ill-informed campaign against him," from D. Murray (2021).

[11] Peterson (2017).

[12] Historically, it is important to log the remarkable maxim from Jonathan Rutherford. He published his landmark monograph, *After Identity*, in 2007. He stated that "we live in an afterlife of the postmodern and post-industrial," (London: Lawrence and Wishart, 2007), p. 9. Clearly, in 2007, the postmodern and post-industrial, with or without the hyphens, were dead concepts. Significantly, Rutherford also realized that, "In the last thirty years, the increasing influences of markets and neo-liberal ideology have transformed the social category of the individual," p. 19. Rutherford, one decade before the Peterson 'moment' was able to show how commodification had summoned an inflated, atomized, marketized, individualized identity.

Foucault, are neoliberal or conservative in their political views.[13] David Burston in his 2020 book *Psychoanalysis, politics and the postmodern university* presented a clear-headed rendering of the Jordan Peterson moment. He asked.

> So is Peterson really a 'public intellectual,' as Paglia (and others) claim? Or is he really just a Right-wing celebrity and culture warrior? Peterson would only be described as a 'public intellectual' if his scholarship was up to scratch. And in this respect, I fear, Peterson does not compare to Canada's best and brightest.[14]

That is a clear, precise and cutting statement. Further, Burston stated that, "fame is going to Peterson's head"[15] and he is a "thinking man's version of Anne Coulter or Rush Limbaugh."[16] There is—indeed—nothing to see here. It is important to present the facts about Jordan Peterson as a researcher. To configure this data set, I have used Google Scholar. This site has been selected with intent. Of all the metrics, it is most generous to academics, in terms of the harvested publications and the citations discovered and logged. In Peterson's case, it includes his doctoral dissertation from McGill, which received no citations, alongside his books in their multiple translations and editions. This list confirms 131 publications, encompassing books reprinted in multiple languages, theses, refereed articles and book chapters. Of these 131 publications spanning from 1990 to 2021, he is first author on 21 and sole author on 16.

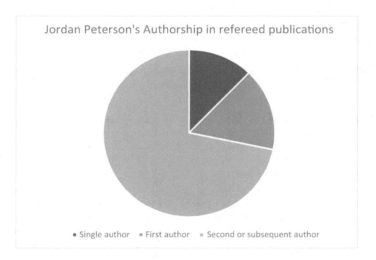

Jordan Peterson's Authorship in refereed publications

■ Single author   ■ First author   ■ Second or subsequent author

---

[13] Zamora and Behrent (2016).

[14] Burston (2020).

[15] ibid., p. 149.

[16] ibid., p. 153.

I have been generous in both the first author and single author measurements. Jordan Peterson has written (only) three single-authored scholarly monographs.[17] The 'scholarly' nature of the two iterations of *12 Rules* is contestable. But to be generous in my calculations, these self-help, trade books have been included. What is significant when reviewing the entire Google Scholar profile is that Peterson has occupied the 'freeloading postdoc' role in publications throughout his career, far transcending his postdoctoral years. Even in the author introduction to *Beyond Order: 12 More Rules for Life*, his academic profile has been described as follows: "with his students and colleagues, Dr Peterson has published over a hundred scientific papers."[18] As with all co-authored publications, it is never clear about the role of each individual researcher. However, for Peterson, in a discipline known for high publication volumes and high citations, he occupies minor authorship roles for the bulk of his research outputs.

A public intellectual, let alone a critical or organic intellectual, must have demonstrated the capacity to be a self-starter, create new knowledge and produce new research. His international profile should attract large groups of PhD students. The nature of clinical psychology is that many 'freeloading postdoc' positions are available on refereed publications.[19] As with medical science more generally, citation rates are high because of the volume of papers cited and the number of researchers on each paper. What researchers see in the case of Jordan Peterson, noting that he runs an individual clinical practice and not a lab where the last author position would be significant, is a high frequency of positioning in the second or third ranking in the authorship hierarchy. This is important. With so few publications outside of self-help 'scholarly monographs' and their translations, and his doctoral thesis, Peterson's capacity to develop a research project from the design through to the dissemination as an individual scholar is not demonstrated or confirmed. Indeed,

---

[17] Oddly, Mikhaila Peterson 'forgot' about *Maps of Meaning* in her review of her father's success. She stated, "His first book sold almost six-million copies. His newer book *Beyond Order* is out March 2, and has pre-sold over 100,000 copies," from M. Peterson (2021). Significantly, the scholarly monograph, based on his course at the University of Toronto, has been erased from history to focus on the non-academic, self-help books.

[18] "Author's Introduction," Peterson (2021).

[19] It is important to note that research integrity protocols and principles have been increasingly governed and regulated during Jordan Peterson's career. It is now more difficult to sustain a 'freeloading postdoc' position in research. The Vancouver Protocol from the International Committee of Medical Journal Editors (http://www.icmje.org/recommendations/browse/roles-and-responsibilities/defining-the-role-of-authors-and-contributors.html) is one such example. Another example is the Australian Code for the Responsible Conduct of Research, 2018, https://www.nhmrc.gov.au/about-us/publications/australian-code-responsible-conduct-research-2018. This matter of authorship is so serious that publishers such as Springer now demand a statement of authorship, https://www.springer.com/cda/content/document/cda_downloaddocument/Authorship+and+disclosure+form+JRS+13.pdf?SGWID=0-0-45-1428379-p173676405. The reason such imperatives exist is because 'courtesy' authorship, particularly between PhD students and their supervisors, has been assumed, resulting in a minimization of student work, but a highly inflated publishing list from supervisors. Noting the recent movements to 'mass authorship'—with thousands of authors for medical articles in particular—the politics of authorship and the validity of research remains an important area to watch, monitor and verify.

his (rare) individual publications, such as "A psycho-ontological analysis of Genesis 2–6," published in the *Archive for the Psychology of Religion*, does not demonstrate ontological, theological or textual rigour.[20] Because he has no expertise in content analysis, thematic analysis or other modes of textual analysis, the 'reading' is arbitrary and non-repeatable.

My scholarly point here is—I know—missing the point. As Paul Wong argued, Peterson, "refuses to play the traditional academic game of research and publications in refereed journals, and yet he is able to achieve greater success through mastering social media."[21] I agree with Wong's analysis. Yet this 'success' is based on the supposed scholarly nature of his academic life. The rationale and understanding of his moment of fame and spotlight remains important to consider. What this evaluation of his research publications confirms is that the left needed strategies to reveal these contradictions and ontological inadequacies, rather than becoming mired in micromoments of aggression and victimhood. To address this concern, it is necessary to move beyond identity politics. It is necessary to talk about refereed research. The difficulty is that myriad issues are crushed into the Jordan Peterson mash: culture wars, safe spaces, victim culture,[22] grievance culture and freedom of speech. When these different issues are forked together into a tasteless glob of sludge, the only possible distinctions that exist are between white people and the rest, white men and the rest, and North America and the rest. As an example, Bradley Campbell and Jason Manning, in their book *The Rise of Victimhood Culture*, state that

> The opposition arises because microaggression complaints violate many longstanding social norms, such as those encouraging people to have a thick skin, brush off slights, and charitably interpret the intentions of others.[23]

The question is why freedom of speech is used as a baton to affirm the right to express racism, homophobia and sexism. This is not a grievance culture. Freedom of speech could be used as a mantra to discuss the poems of Wordsworth, Patti LaBelle's voice or the tunings of Keith Richards. Indeed, freedom of speech could be used to discuss the black market in ivory trading, the privatization of water or habitat security for orangutans in Kalimantan. Instead, the focus is on the right to use flags from the confederacy, validate histories of slavery, or 'slut shaming.' Indeed, if a person wishes to attack the body or skin colour of another, they have the right to do so. The greater question—not answered or even addressed by Campbell and Manning— is why critics on the right justify the time, the air space and currency granted to these personal attacks. They may be microaggressions. They may configure a victim. They may create a culture of grievance. But why are discussions focused on individuals and their skin colour, body shape or genitalia? Who—actually—cares? Are these issues a priority for our public discussion in our present? Individuals have a right to

---

[20] Peterson (2007).

[21] Wong (2019).

[22] Joan Smith studied "an epidemic of violence against women in this country" and located "classic victim-blaming, something often witnessed during outbursts of male violence," from *Home Grown: How domestic violence turns men into terrorists*, (London: Riverrun, 2019), loc 279.

[23] Campbell and Manning (2018).

live a safe and productive life, away from daily assaults on public transport, in the workplace or on the street. Therefore, there are two parts to this issue: (1) why it is necessary to abuse and label the personhood of another, requiring them to have a 'thick skin' and (2) why do public and academic discourses remain focused on the personal and the private, rather than creating a heightened dialogue to make freedom of speech meaningful? Indeed, it is made meaningful by being based on the freedom to read widely, the freedom to think, the freedom to be silent and the freedom to listen. Instead, there is a confusion of freedom of speech with a demand to be heard, the right to a large audience, the capacity to make statements without debate or questioning, and the capacity to express misogyny without a feminist commentary.

The left requires a vision of and for the world. My book continues to return to this issue. These problems, errors and over-stepping beyond Peterson's scholarly expertise were confirmed in his 2022 Spotify podcast with Joe Rogan where - in a single interview - Peterson confused weather and climate science, race-based categories and subjective opinions on skin colour, and his feelings about music, rather than accessing musicological research (Rogan and Peterson 2022). Such over-statements are not new. He demonstrates the confidence of a meth addict on a scrag, and this attitude is best captured in one oft-repeated phrase: "Postmodern NeoMarxists."[24] This phrase is gibberish. His repetition of this odd compound noun does not render it any less inane, ignorant and foolish. It is clear and obvious that Jordan Peterson does not understand Marxism or postmodernism. That is not debateable. The greater question—the crucial question—is probing the role of these words for his audiences. How are Jordan Peterson's fans/followers/supporters interpellated through these words? When they are used, what do they hear? This may be part of what Laclau and Mouff explored in their theories of populism through the summoning of an imaginary enemy against which followers can align. Through the proliferation of information sources, a multiplicity of different forces conflict and dance and agitate to speak on the behalf of 'the people.' This is Jordan Peterson's strategy, to activate and weaponize words and phrases like freedom, equality and free speech. These ideas gain fire and a frame through the summoning of the inelegant and inaccurate phrase, "Postmodern NeoMarxists."[25] These Postmodern NeoMarxists are stopping decent, ethical, and mediocre men from passing off their opinions, biases and subjectivities as the truths that fuel our culture.

The difficulty when managing populist techniques is that they are slippery. It is difficult to argue against freedom. Matthew McManus—like Zizek—enacted a service to the international academy in his 2020 book, *The rise of post-modern conservatism*.[26] McManus demonstrated the movement of postmodernism beyond specialist theorists and into the vocabulary of xenophobic nationalists and Alt-Right narratives. There are many reasons why the left faced challenges engaging with and critiquing Peterson's use of the phrase. The primary explanation is that most of us in the humanities have not been in a seminar mentioning postmodernism

---

[24] Peterson (2017).

[25] ibid.

[26] McManus (2020).

since—in my case—1992.[27] My late husband Professor Steve Redhead wrote a book titled—following on from Latour, *We have never been postmodern.*[28] There is no singular postmodern philosophy because there are multiple modernities and engagements with it. Therefore, as McManus has shown—as postmodernism moved from specialist use to political battleaxe, it was emptied of meaning and weaponized by the right.

Jordan Peterson was not alone in using words he did not have the training, research expertise or peer reviewed verification to summon and deploy. In a post-expertise age, many of these issues are caused by academics either speaking outside of their research focus and offering an opinion ungrounded in the field, or not communicating their research beyond their discipline, with careful and subtle attention to considered dissemination. Many of the words used by Peterson have a huge literature encircling them. He did not read that literature and was able to blather about with words as weapons rather than as accurate tools for the configuration of an argument. To critique his use of these terms is difficult, because there are vast libraries of specialist reading that he has completely ignored.

I understand the frustration in attempting to manage ignorance of this scale. Where would we start with the critique? The danger is that Jordan Peterson—without rapid and expert dispersion of his bizarre, inelegant and incorrect arguments—has calcified his commentary, calling for humanities departments to be closed because of all the "Postmodern NeoMarxists"[29] (that do not exist). This is academic Punch and Judy. Such statements become even more troubling when read through his political lens. As Peterson stated, "a lot of what determines your political orientation is biological temperament, far more than people realise."[30] Therefore, the lesson from the Post Peterson paradigm is scholars must ensure that we do not confuse our disciplinary expertise with wider expertise in higher education studies. Most of the academics who work in a university do not study it historically or sociologically as an institution. It is a workplace. Therefore, scholars must create languages and strategies to intervene— with precision—in such debates. These debates may burn out as is the case with Peterson, but ensuring that the academic use of social media is clean, clear, considered and points to refereed scholarship remains key.

Nonsense must be dispatched and critiqued at each turn. For example, Annette Poizner's *From Chaos to Order: A guide to Jordan Peterson's worldview*, published in 2020, described his work as "seminal and important"[31] and confirms that—breathe with me, dear reader—"the postmodernism he discusses strongly influences the

---

[27] My experience was confirmed by Brett Nicholls who stated that, "it is widely held within academic circles today that the term 'postmodernism' is unclear, overtly complicated and, perhaps, passe. Scholars who cut their academic teeth on this complex thought in the 1980 and 1990s now supervise doctoral students who have little or no use for it," from R. Overall and B. Nichols (2020).

[28] Redhead (2011).

[29] Peterson (2017).

[30] Peterson (2019).

[31] Poizner (2020).

mental health fields."[32] It gets worse. She argues, "Peterson suggests that your basic premises about reality, likely influenced by the way that science has advanced our lives, may be wrong."[33] This is an example of the problem. Peterson was inaccurate, flawed and had not researched the terms he was using. Because his ignorance was not dispatched and critiqued with rigour and speed, writers with even less knowledge than him jumped the shark. The wrongness amplifies. Another book—edited by Ron Dart and titled *Myth and meaning in Jordan Peterson: a Christian perspective*, revealed the supposed problems with science and knowledge,[34] and Peterson touches "the deeper longing in the human heart."[35] Anti-empirical, anti-theory and anti-fact, religious faith provides the meaning system required for this unsettled time where those in power are teetering in their authority and capacity to command, dominate and rule without question, history or context. Jim Proser continued the starkly incorrect presentation of postmodernism summoned by Peterson, describing it as "a hit in academia, where university administrators were always keen to accommodate their young customers and prospects. The utopian promise of Marxism, at the core of postmodernism, was the rage."[36] The—where-is-the-nearest-yoga-class-so-I-can-meditate—ludicrousness of "university administrators" valuing postmodernism because it is popular is the equivalent level of fantasy to Q-Anon confirming that John F. Kennedy is still alive and living in Russia. This is what Zizek described as Peterson's "art of lying with truth."[37] His followers simplify the process. They lie with lies.

Beyond the echoing lies, one interpretation of Jordan Peterson is that his version of self-help has—as the label suggests—helped people. Clement Sibanda confirmed that he, "changed my destructive behaviour and set me on the path to a meaningful life and spiritual growth."[38] While such scaffolding can be personally liberating, there are consequences if opinions replace research. For example, Sibanda's advice for those also seeking meaning and spirituality is, "skip dating. Go straight to courtship. You will date when married."[39] Considering the complex socio-sexual negotiations within heterosexuality at the moment, what is required is care, conversations and time. Courtship belongs in the TARDIS, summoning corsets and costume dramas. But what is clear is that there is a burgeoning group of books emerging that take Jordon Peterson's simple ideas, simplifies them further, and self publishes the results. This is like eating a hot dog, without the hot dog. Yes, Jordan Peterson's hot dog was made from poor quality meat. But this simplified version is composed of a day-old

---

[32] ibid., p. 2.

[33] ibid., p. 4.

[34] Dart (2020).

[35] ibid., p. 5.

[36] Proser (2020).

[37] Zizek (2020).

[38] Sibanda (2020).

[39] ibid., p. 13.

bun, limp lettuce and an unrecognizable vegetable that may be a tomato. It is many things. It is not a hot dog.

It is understandable that in an era where work, family, housing and food are insecure, and politicians pick irrelevant or unsubstantial issues to emphasize and fetishize, that there would be a desire to return to order, rules and the past. However, those orders, rules and the past were based on the oppression, suppression and exploitation of the majority. Neither Christianity nor capitalism—neither communism nor atheism—can wash the blood of injustice from the cloth of international history. But education, learning, reading and thinking can be transformative and summon "epistemological ethics."[40] However simply because we use water does not mean we are an expert plumber. Simply because a person works in a university does not mean the speaker has any knowledge in the history and policy environment of higher education. Experience is not expertise. Jordan Peterson is one of many academics that assume because they lecture in a university that they hold an understanding of teaching and learning. The overwhelming majority of university academics hold no teaching qualifications. Their 'curriculum' is a result of disciplinary ability mashed with assumptions about student learning. Similarly, the majority of academics will never occupy leadership roles. They watch leaders and critique their actions. Yet they do not have the courage or the gumption to step into these difficult positions, make tough decisions and grind out a result in times of declining funding and belief in education.[41] The fundamental contradictions of academic life are—indeed—unsustainable. Teaching colonizes our professional and personal lives. Promotion is enacted through research. Leadership selection emerges from the already existing pod of senior staff. Therefore, academic leaders are selected from the sciences, where the metrics of research are verified through tiers of journals and citation factors for refereed articles, rather than publishing scholarly monographs and developing long-term readerships. Indeed, research 'success' results in teaching responsibilities being 'bought out' by grants. When leadership opportunities are available, the best fit remains men in the empirical sciences with a research track record confirmed through metrics, because teaching excellence (let alone expertise in configuring learning cultures) is so much more difficult to measure.

The housework of universities—first year teaching, pastoral care and learning-led committee work—remains dominated by women. This is the current reality that Jordan Peterson's critique of the university merely reinforces. Indeed, Jordan Peterson reclaims and resummons the reality presented by Adrienne Rich in 1979.

---

[40] Michelson (2019).

[41] This point was explored by Paul James in "Cruel irony or structural cruelty? How good people are destroying our universities," *Arena*, August 13, 2020. He stated that, "we do not need hard-edged neoliberals to do it to us: academic managers can be calmy efficient about the process, and, despite an articulate and active critical minority, many academics have over the last couple of decades quietly allowed it to happen with little sustained response."

What we have at present is a man-centered university, a breeding ground not of humanism but of masculine privilege. As women have gradually and reluctantly been admitted into the mainstream of higher education, they have been made participants in a system that prepares men to take up roles of power in a man-centered society, that asks questions and teaches 'facts' generated by a male intellectual tradition, and that both subtly and openly confirms men as the leaders and shapers of human destiny both within and outside academia.[42]

While the academic participation of women as students and scholars has increased since this essay was published, women remain strongly under-represented in senior academic roles, and there is a salary gap between men and women.[43] But significantly, in the context of understanding Jordan Peterson, Adrienne Rich's configuration of the distinguished male professor—surrounded by women including a wife, students, assistants and secretaries—remains stark and resonant.

It is easy to complain from a safe and tenured North American academic post. But clinical psychology is not an effective discipline or approach to understand all knowledge, including the history of the university. Peterson's specialisms in abnormal, social and personality psychology are not generalizable to other disciplines that operate in higher education. A man who has never worked or researched outside of elite institutions has no grasp of the role of higher education in regional development, health policy or school leadership. An opinion is not expertise. Working in a university does not mean it is understood.

References

Acker, S., Webber, M., & Smyth, E. (2016). Continuity or change? Gender, family and academic work for junior faculty in Ontario Universities. *NASPA Journal about Women in Higher Education, 9*(1), 1–20.

Burston, D. (2020). *Psychoanalysis, politics and the postmodern university* (p. xii). Palgrave.

Campbell, B., & Manning, J. (2018). *The rise of victimhood culture: Microaggressions, safe spaces, and the new culture wars*. Macmillan.

Dart, R. (2020). *Myth and meaning in Jordan Peterson: A Christian perspective*. Lexham Press.

Hartley, L. (1958). *The go-between*. Penguin.

McManus, M. (2020). *The rise of post-modern conservatism: Neoliberalism, post-modern culture, and reactionary politics*. Gewerbestrasse: Palgrave.

Michelson, E. (2019). The ethical knower: Rethinking our pedagogy in the age of Trump. *Adult Education Quarterly, 69*(2), 142–156.

Murray, D. (2021, 1 September). Farewell to Cambridge's disastrous Vice-Chancellor. *The Spectator*. https://www.spectator.co.uk/article/farewell-to-cambridge-s-disastrous-vice-chancellor.

Overall, R., & Nichols, B (Eds.). (2020). *Post-Truth and the mediation of reality: New conjunctures*, p. 57. Springer.

Peterson, J. (2017, 10 July). Postmodern Neomarxism: Diagnosis and cure. *Jordan B Peterson YouTube*. https://www.youtube.com/watch?v=s4c-jOdPTN8.

Peterson, J. (1999). *Maps of meaning: The architecture of belief* (p. xi). Routledge.

Peterson, J. (2007). A psycho-ontological analysis of Genesis 2–6. *Archive for the Psychology of Religion, 29*(1), 87–12.

---

[42] Rich (1979).

[43] Acker et al. (2016).

Peterson, J. (2017, 10 July). Postmodern Neomarxism: Diagnosis and cure. *Jordan B Peterson YouTube*. https://www.youtube.com/watch?v=s4c-jOdPTN8.

Peterson, J. (2021). *Beyond order: 12 More rules for life* (p. 30). Penguin.

Peterson, J. (2021). *Beyond order: 12 More rules for life* (p. 17). Penguin.

Peterson, J. (2022). Why I am no longer a tenured professor at the University of Toronto. *National Post*. https://nationalpost.com/opinion/jordan-peterson-why-i-am-no-longer-a-tenured-professor-at-the-university-of-toronto

Peterson, M. (2021, 1 March). How we built the Jordan Peterson media empire. *National Post*. https://nationalpost.com/news/canada/mikhaila-peterson-how-we-built-the-jordan-peterson-media-empire.

Peterson, J. (2021). *Beyond order: 12 More rules for life*, p. v. London: Penguin.

Peterson, J. (2022). Why I am no longer a tenured professor at the University of Toronto. *National Post*. https://nationalpost.com/opinion/jordan-peterson-why-i-am-no-longer-a-tenured-professor-at-the-university-of-toronto

Poizner, A. (2020). *From chaos to order: A guide to Jordan Peterson's worldview* (p. 1). Lobster University Press.

Proser, J. (2020). *Savage messiah* (p. 289). New York: St Martin's Press.

Proser, J. (2020). *Savage Messiah*, p. 29. New York: St Martin's Press.

Redhead, S. (2011). *We have never been postmodern*. Edinburgh University Press.

Rich, A. (1979). "Toward a woman-centered university", from *On Lies, Secrets and Silence: Selected Prose 1966–1978* (p. 127). W.W. Norton.

Richards, S. (2017). *The rise of the outsiders: How mainstream politics lost its way* (p. 1). Atlantic.

Rogan, J., & Peterson, J. (2022). #1769-Jordan Peterson. *The Joe Rogan Experience*. https://open.spotify.com/episode/7IVFm4085auRaIHS7N1NQl

Sibanda, C. (2020). *Transcending Chaos: 12 Other Rules from Jordan Peterson*. Self-published, p. 3.

Wong, P. (2019). Assessing Jordan B. Peterson's contribution to the psychology of wellbeing. *International Journal of Wellbeing, 9*(1), 83–102.

Zamora, D., & Behrent, M. (Eds.), *Foucault and neoliberalism*. Cambridge: Polity.

Zizek, S. (2020). Jordan Peterson as a symptom of … What? In B. Burgis, C. Hamilton, M. McManus, & M. Trejo (Eds.), *Myth and Mayhem: A leftist critique of Jordan Peterson*, p. 1. Winchester: Zero Books.

Chapter 8
Rule 7–Freedom to read is more important than freedom of speech

Free speech. Compelled speech. Cancel culture.[1] No platform. These phrases feed into a series of debates that summon ignorance, disrespect, rudeness, foolishness and incompetence. If a person has a thought and wishes to express it, then that is a choice they can make. However, if slander or defamation follows, there will be consequences. All of the heat about free speech and compelled speech that propelled Jordan Peterson to notoriety on the matter of trans rights and the nouns applied to humans is not the key issue or the problem. Indeed, it is the mask for the issue.

While all the attention is place on freedom of speech, how about we focus our time, energy and respect on the freedom to read so that when speech does emerge, it is informed rather than ignorant, it is research-based rather than reactive, and framed by expertise rather than experience.[2] Jordan Peterson offered his supposed protest in response to Bill C-16, which he described as thought regulation and "compelled speech."[3] It was neither of these cultural forces, as university officials, professors of jurisprudence and lawyers have confirmed. Since 2016, his desire to express misogynistic ideas and undermine trans communities, languages and presence is the truth that lives and breathes amid these lies. The *New York Times* described him as "the

---

[1] I will reference and log one of the most troubling of the 'cancel culture' texts, noting the wide and expanding literature encircling this phrase. Written by Alexander Reich, *Cancel Culture: how to thrive in a culture that has given up on masculinity, femininity, sex, success, god and a great life*, (self-published, 2020), this book confirms the "general decline in testosterone," p. 74. He also confirms that "women, are actually closer to animals," p. 102. Reich offers, "an important fact about women. Women are almost 90% malleable in their behavior," p. 110. These odd and unverified comments continue with such statements as "foreplay these days is literally just watching porn together," p. 139. This book is what emerges when a 30-year-old man attends the gym, looks at himself in the mirror and writes a blog that (very) few other 30-year-old men—who also look in the mirror a lot—think is 'cool.' This book is what emerges when an under-educated man reads the Wikipedia entry for Sparta and decides he has discovered the model for his own life - and the rest of us.

[2] I also note the issue of valuing freedom in any form. As Louis Althusser stated, "the individual is interpellated as a (free) subject in order that he shall submit freely to the commandments of the Subject, i.e., in order that he shall (freely) accept his subjection," from Althusser (2012).

[3] Peterson (2018).

T. Brabazon, *12 Rules for (Academic) Life*,
https://doi.org/10.1007/978-981-16-9291-8_8

custodian of the patriarchy."[4] They are right. To cite *Maps of Meaning*, Peterson's first monograph,

> The properly structured patriarchal system fulfills the needs of the present while taking into account those of the future; simultaneously, it balances the demands of the self with those of the other.

As revealed through this oddly aphoristic statement, Peterson treats himself very seriously, which only enhances *The Goon Show*-like tendency of his prose. When he speaks with phrases like "Postmodern NeoMarxists,"[5] he reveals a profound truth of our culture: freedom to speak is not as important as the freedom to read. This Peterson moment also confirms—in an era where power and authority have been abused and defiled and leadership is as rare as a unicorn—that the only possible appeals are to an imagined past of invented traditions and safety. In such times, critical theory is required. Desperately. But this theory must connect with social and political conditions. Theorists must hook and frame their ideas into contemporary life, to provide a clear, intelligent, transparent set of arguments to counter the under-researched opinions of another dissatisfied and angry white man in a suit, shielding pseudo-religious self-help within the prophylactic of research. To confirm this point, Peterson in *Beyond Order: 12 More Rules for Life*, presented the following:

> Question: Who are you – or, at least, who could you be? Answer: Part of the eternal force that constantly confronts the terrible unknown, voluntarily.[6]

This is an Oprahfied version of scholarship. Put another way, this is the banal masquerading as the significant. Indeed, it is the petulant offering profundity.

Reading is so much more important than speaking. To use one of the few scholars Peterson mentions in his "Postmodern NeoMarxist"[7] waterfall of ignorance, let us summon Michel Foucault.[8] In *The Order of Things* by Foucault, he does not discuss Marxist economic theory. Instead, Adam Smith is cited alongside presentations of liberal models of economics. The reason the French scholar made this theoretical selection was because—and this statement is derived from Foucault—"Marxism exists in nineteenth century thought like a fish in water; that is, it is unable to breathe anywhere else."[9] Further, strong research emerged after Foucault's death confirming his affinity for neoliberalism late in his career.[10] If Marxist critiques were required, where is Hannah Arendt's research cited in Peterson's critique of Marxist theorizations of totalitarianism?[11] Similarly with all the attention on compelled speech and blockages to his freedom of speech, there was no attention to why C-16 emerged.

---

[4] Bowles (2018).

[5] Peterson (2017b).

[6] Peterson (2021a).

[7] Peterson (2017b).

[8] Peterson (2017c).

[9] Foucault (1970).

[10] Zamora and Behrent (2016).

[11] Arendt (1994).

Laws exist in context, as decades of socio-legal theory confirm. Mary Ellen Donnan, in her remarkable book, *The Shattered Mosaic: how Canadian social structures cause homelessness*, published in 2016—the year of the Peterson dummy spit—confirmed that 10% of the youth population is lesbian, gay, bisexual, trans and non-binary. But this community composes 25–40% of the youth homeless population.[12] A 2017 study in the *Archives of Neuropsychiatry* demonstrated that 29.8% of the study of 99 transmen and 42 transwomen[13] had attempted suicide at least once.[14] This is a small study. Generalizability is difficult to determine or sustain. But silence is not an option in understanding suicide and homelessness amongst the trans population. Freedom of speech is the least of the social problems to consider. It is important to hear, affirm and summon the words of Professor A W Peet, Professor Physics at the University of Toronto. They confirmed, "I think it's about abuse of power. Peterson is using his position as a university professor to build his revenue stream ... He took the life force from me and some of our students and dehumanized us for fun and profit and I'm still not ok with it."[15] Neither should we be. Certainly, there are white, heterosexual men, living in North America that have suffered profound inequalities, loss and injustice. Yet the flaw in Peterson's argument emerges when he blames the uncertainty and confusion experienced by these white men onto women, people of colour and the trans community. This YouTube-carried patriarchy displaces important areas for discussion and commentary, using the puppets of narcissism[16] and projection.

Research is the key to this conversation. Speech is of trailing relevance. Therefore, after demonstrating the misstep with Peterson's reading of Foucault, it is time to assess Jordan Peterson's use of Jean Baudrillard, supposedly the great postmodernist. I have read and deployed Baudrillard for thirty years. During this time, one truth has emerged. 'Scholars' or citizens that throw Baudrillard into the postmodern rubbish bin have not read Baudrillard. Even at the height of his fame as a 'postmodern theorist,' Baudrillard was mobilizing Aristotle's phronesis, not refuting science, but recognizing the value of empirical methods and the data sets created from them.[17] However he also confirmed that those results cannot be moved to any societal context and assume they are valid and meaningful. Therefore, the assumption that gender and sexuality—two volatile terms—are stable, standardized and ahistorical is incorrect. Baudrillard was never against science or empirical methods. He argued that we must understand science in the context of the object of study. Put another way, why is one

---

[12] Donnan (2016).

[13] Please note: it is not conventional or preferred practice to refer to 'transmen' and 'transwomen.' Men and women are the accurate identifiers. However, this study wished to focus on the trans community and the gendering within it. I respect the terms of the original study, while noting the foundation importance of recognizing men, women and non-binary citizens.

[14] Yuksel et al. (2017).

[15] Peet and Chiose (2017).

[16] Manne (2014).

[17] Baudrillard (2005).

area of research funded and not another? That is not a science question. That is a cultural question.

Baudrillard's reversibility is the key moment and intervention in sexual politics. Instead of gender (femininity) being predicated on sex (female), what if sex is predicated on gender? That was the great Judith Butler's project.[18] At its most basic, the Butler argument is that in life I do not walk around seeing clitorises and penises. This is not my lived experience. I do not need to see a penis to assume masculinity. These assumptions may be wrong. But we—as readers of bodies—make judgements every day on the basis of a haircut, lipstick, shoe selection and fabric. These assumptions are made without seeing a penis, or the absence of a penis. These assumptions are about the viewer reading the body, rather than the body itself. As Butler stated, "gender is … instituted in an exterior space through a stylized repetition of acts."[19] Reading such research permits the gift of insight. Instead, Peterson makes a leap between science and rationality and truth, and assumes there is a truth below an illusion. Perhaps the illusion is real.[20] Perhaps many of us—each day—make assumptions about identity based on little more than our personal history and the wearing of mascara. We look at the surface of a body and make decisions. Identity is an epistemological moisturiser, building up cultures on the layers of the skin.

The spaces between feminism and postmodernism are complex, convoluted and require close and considered reading. If Peterson wanted to explore this space, Derrida, Foucault and Baudrillard were not effective guides. Judith Butler would have been appropriate. So would Sara Ahmed, who published a book in 1998 titled *Differences that matter: Feminist theory and postmodernism*. It is a tough book with a complex introduction, in which she acknowledges: "it is difficult to begin writing a book with a sense of anticipation that one's reader may already be feeling a sense of dread."[21] If Peterson wanted evidence for the difficult and intricate academic conversations about postmodernism—which he would read as "Postmodern NeoMarxist"[22]—then Sara Ahmed's, 1998 monograph would provide an evidential base. Asking "where is postmodernism?"[23] this book added a post to postmodernism, confirming the ending of this theoretical moment, noting its lack of generalizability and exclusivity. If Peterson required a straw harpy to enable his attack on difficult women writing difficult research, then Sara Ahmed's early book

---

[18] Butler (2002).

[19] ibid., p. 41.

[20] As Jean Baudrillard confirmed, "at all events, illusion is indestructible. The world as it is—which is not at all the 'real world'—perpetually eludes the investigation of meaning, thus causing the present catastrophe of the apparatus of production of the 'real world,' so true is it that illusion cannot be combatted with truth—that is merely to redouble the illusion—but only be a higher illusion," from *The Perfect Crime*, (New York: Verso, 2008).

[21] Ahmed (1998).

[22] Peterson (2017b).

[23] Ahmed, *op. cit.*, p. 8.

would have provided a provocative footnote.[24] Instead, because he has not read her work, he reverts back to the incorrect 'citations' of Foucault and Derrida.

In case you, dear reader, wish to hurtle the "Postmodern NeoMarxist"[25] Peterson playbook at me when I offer such commentary, it is important to summon Nietzsche in this skirmish. He is often mentioned by Peterson, but without depth or interpretation, Nietzsche was clear about the chimera and fog that winks at the truth.

> What then is truth? A mobile army of metaphors, metonyms—in short, a sum of human relations, which have been enhanced, transposed, and embellished poetically and rhetorically, and which after long use seem firm, canonical, and obligatory to the people: truths are illusions about which one has forgotten that is what they are.[26]

This statement is not made by Baudrillard. It is from Nietzsche. Reading widely and conducting research is transformative because it creates ontological complexity, historical awareness, debate and interpretation. Instead, Peterson reads the Bible, Jung, Solzhenitsyn and Dostoyevsky. This is not the most robust or expansive of reference lists. The repetitive mention of science, which seemingly slots into empiricism, is not meaningful. Peterson stated to Sam Harris, "The claim I'm making is that scientific truth is nested inside moral truth, and moral truth is the final adjudicator (Peterson in Harris 2017)." This is behaviouralism cloaked in belief, welcoming a morality of punishment and reward.

Reading requires that we move outside of our personal experience, our limitations or singular epistemological lens. The strength of not reading—of ignorance—is that Jordan Peterson can ignore research so that white men residing in North American can continue to live a comfortable life.[27] Truth, morality and science: these words are weaponized for Peterson. It is possible to study theology and not be a Christian. It is possible to use Marxist tools and not be a Marxist. Marxist theories can be used to critique Stalin's Soviet Union, Thatcher's Britain, Muldoon's New Zealand or Trump's America. They can be used to think about predatory capitalism, real estate capitalism and finance capitalism. Instead, Peterson instructed us to, "Clean up your room."[28] This statement is hard to argue against, but what of the intellectual commentary? How can we be against making a bed? Making a bed is a good idea. But with all his education and research, is making a bed the best public intellectual expertise he has to share?

---

[24] To probe a review of Sara Ahmed's career please refer to T. Brabazon, A. Cornelius-Bell and E. Armstrong (2021). This article also contains links to the Sara Ahmed weekly reading series, exploring the monographs published through her career. This close mode of research with significant scholars demonstrates the granular detail and analysis required for considered critique.

[25] Peterson (2017b).

[26] Nietzsche (1976).

[27] I note rule 8—"Try to make one room in your home as beautiful as possible." This rule comes from J. Peterson (2021b).

[28] Peterson (2017a).

An alternative focus is a discussion that the richest 0.1% of Americans have increased their share of wealth from 7% in the 1970s to 22% in the 2010s.[29] Further, the top 0.1% are worth more in the United States—financially—than the bottom 90%. Still the focus is on an individual making a bed. Therefore, in his moment of fame, he was wrong, irrational and misleading. He lacked precision. He built a career on posturing, not reading.

References

Ahmed, S. (1998). *Differences that matter: Feminist theory and postmodernism* (p. 1). Cambridge University Press.

Althusser, L. (2012). *On the reproduction of capitalism: Ideology and ideological state apparatus.* Verso.

Baudrillard, J. (2005). *The intelligence of evil: Or the lucidity pact.* Bloomsbury.

Bowles, N., & Peterson, J. (2018, 18 May). Custodian of the Patriarchy, *New York Times.* https://www.nytimes.com/2018/05/18/style/jordan-peterson-12-rules-for-life.html.

Brabazon, T., Cornelius-Bell, A., Armstrong, E. (2021). The pandemic PhD programme. *International Journal of Social Sciences and Educational Studies, 8*(4), 165–188. https://ijsses.tiu.edu.iq/index.php/volume-8-issue-2-article-14/.

Butler, J. (2002). *Gender trouble.* Routledge.

Donnan, M. (2016). *The shattered mosaic: How Canadian social structures cause homelessness.* Charton Publishing.

Foucault, M. (1970). *The order of things,* p. 262. London, Tavistock.

Harris, S., & Peterson, J. (2017) *Waking Up Podcast What is True? A Conversation with Jordan B.* Peterson. https://pdfcoffee.com/sam-harris-jordan-b-peterson-what-is-truth-transcript-pdf-free.html

Manne, A. (2014). *The life of I: The new culture of narcissism.* Melbourne University Press.

Nietzsche, F. (1976). *Portable Nietzsche* (p. 46). Viking.

Peet, A. W., & Chiose, S. (2017, 2 June). Jordan Peterson and the trolls in the ivory tower. *The Globe and Mail.* https://www.theglobeandmail.com/news/national/education/jordan-peterson-university-of-toronto-free-speech-crowdfunding/article35174379/.

Peterson, J. (2018, 28 March). The Queen's university talk: The rising tide of compelled speech, *Jordan B. Peterson YouTube.* https://www.youtube.com/watch?v=MwdYpMS8s28.

Peterson, J. (2017a, 15 May) Clean up your room. *Bite-sized philosophy. YouTube.* https://www.youtube.com/watch?v=BBR5v89L6gk.

Peterson, J. (2017b, 10 July). Postmodern Neomarxism: Diagnosis and cure. *Jordan B Peterson YouTube.* https://www.youtube.com/watch?v=s4c-jOdPTN8.

Peterson, J. (2017c). Foucault the reprehensible & Derrida the trickster. *Bite-sized Philosophy.* https://www.youtube.com/watch?v=NBFSDd_5tiE.

Peterson, J. (2021a). *Beyond order: 12 more rules for life* (p. 198). Penguin.

Peterson, J. (2021b). *Beyond order: 12 More rules for life* (p. 57). Penguin.

Yuksel, S., et al. (2017). A clinically neglected topic: Risk of suicide in transgender individuals. *Archives of Neuropsychiatry, 54*(1), 28–32.

Zamora, D., & Behrent, M. (Eds.). (2016). *Foucault and neoliberalism.* Cambridge: Polity.

---

[29] A. Monaghan, US wealth inequality—top 0.1% worth as much as the bottom 90%, *The Guardian*, November 13, 2014, https://www.theguardian.com/business/2014/nov/13/us-wealth-inequality-top-01-worth-as-much-as-the-bottom-90.

Chapter 9
Rule 8–Be a leader, rather than complain about leadership

Leadership is not a role, a title or a pay scale. Leadership is a desire, a motivation, an imperative, a hope and a goal. We do have a crisis of leadership in international higher education, and it is a problem of men. Women are promoted at a slower rate through the ranks in international higher education and they dominate the disciplines that are configured within a STEMified ideology as being secondary, soft, the caring professions and not integral to the knowledge economy. These disciplines include the care of the very young and the very old, educating our citizenry, and developing and managing our service economy, which is the foundation for the knowledge economy. Funding, awards, prizes and attention are moved towards STEM—Science, Technology, Engineering and Mathematics—and this shift has consequences to politics, public discourse, management and leadership.

In the United States, women composed 31% of full-time faculty. This figure had increased 5% in the previous 75 years.[1] During this period, women enrolling and graduating from college degrees had tripled.[2] In Australian universities, revealed through DEEWR Higher Education Statistics, 22% of full professors were women and 30% of Vice Chancellors and Deputy Vice Chancellors.[3] A study from Larkins shows that since that DEEWR data set was released, women's employment has increased, with women dominating the teaching only appointments in our universities.[4] In the UK, there are three times more male professors than female professors, with only 1% of British professors being black.[5]

Then there is the sex problem. An Independent Commission Against Corruption (ICAC) report, delivered in August 2020, confirmed that the Vice Chancellor of the University of Adelaide, Professor Peter Rathjen, scientist and Vice Chancellor at a Group of 8 institution, which is equivalent to the Ivy League or the Russell Group

---

[1] Turner Kelly (2019).

[2] ibid.

[3] Strachan et al. (2011).

[4] Larkins (2011).

[5] Adams (2020).

in the United States and United Kingdom, had not only sexually harassed women, but then lied about it to the Chancellor and ICAC.[6] The investigators confirmed that this pattern of behaviour had been seen in his previous two posts, at the University of Melbourne and the University of Tasmania, both also elite institutions. Each university supposedly conducted due diligence and found no evidence or pattern in this behaviour. Because this due diligence was activated by believing a man over a woman, Rathjen got away with this behaviour for decades. Yet he is not a bad apple.[7] This is a system that values and validates men to have a career and be promoted on high salaries, with travel benefits and a freedom most of us can never imagine. They then move to another institution when the institution is not as responsive to their needs.

These are heterosexual men. Procreative men. White men. These men are drawn from the disciplines of science and engineering. There is an assumption of competence, of intelligence, of rigour and integrity unless proven otherwise. Anyone outside of this very narrow group must prove their ability. It is very easy to abuse the leadership of universities. Camille Paglia and Jordan Peterson in their conversation[8] fixated on this leadership, and how leaders were separated from 'faculty,' that is academics. Paglia and Peterson blame 'administrators' for the political correctness and compelled speech. Wrong again. But once more, they argued that the entire leadership structure should be removed, which was rather amusing considering that removing university leadership is nihilistic and chaotic, the antithesis to their traditionalism and harking to the past. They are tied in knots of problems through their opinions, that masquerade as research. They critique the number of women graduating from universities. They critique the arts and humanities, disciplines dominated by women. They critique the leadership in higher education, dominated by men from the sciences. Here are two careerist academics, safely tenured and free to express strange, paradoxical, disturbing and contradictory ideas on a regular basis. The question remains, if they were so critical of leadership in our universities, why did they not put their hand up to fulfill these roles? It is so much easier to slam, shame, critique and ridicule. It is so much harder to be present and solve problems and issues, and be an agent for change rather than part of the sludge of stability and conformity.

I do not agree with them. I have studied leadership in our universities for twenty years. Is there poor leadership in our universities? Absolutely. Can we do better? Absolutely. Do we need to do better? Absolutely. Does leadership matter? Absolutely. Therefore, to understand what is happening to render such important roles so banal, incompetent and toxic, it is important to review the last few decades of higher education. Stanley Aronowitz, in 2000, published the dystopic scholarly monograph, *The Knowledge Factory*.[9] It is an incisively accurate presentation of the contemporary university. He argued that that the people entering higher education administration

---

[6] *Statement about an Investigation – University of Adelaide*, Independent Commission Against Corruption, Office of Public Integrity, August 2020, https://icac.sa.gov.au/public-statement/26a ug2020.

[7] Brabazon (2020a).

[8] Peterson et al. (2017).

[9] Aronowitz (2000).

had failed as teachers and researchers. They enter the third stream of management to rule over those who succeeded in spheres where they were weak. While such a portrayal is cruel, we have lived through poor leadership 'facilitating' curricula design that reduces costs and quality, and mediocre researchers telling academics that 'books don't matter.' This intellectual cost is matched by a personal consequence to individual academics. We have also lived through the arbitrariness and carelessness of higher education leadership and the execution of power. Peter Fleming's *Dark Academia* captures the challenges, the pain and the horror of this time.[10]

Noting all these weaknesses, anarcho-syndicalism is not the best option at this point. Neither is deciding between the People's Front of Judea or the Judean People's Front model of leadership, to summon Monty Python. Sometimes, the most political action any of us can do is be present. Occupy the moment. Stand. It is very easy to complain about leadership. I have worked for deans where staff were pushed to suicide under their watch, a Vice Chancellor more interested in their personal wealth than international education, and who sits and watches the abuse cascade before them without an intervention.

It was at this moment that I decided to enter leadership roles. I loved being a teacher and research academic. I taught first year students for 25 years. Research is my passion. But this zombie leadership was not only killing people, but destroying our universities. One person cannot make a difference to a sector, but one person can start a movement or momentum and may save a life at best, or perhaps a career. I decided to enter leadership differently. I still teach and train. I am still research active. This balance is incredibly tough to execute. My last three contracts have been focused completely on 'management', without a single hour for research. I made a deal with myself that I would not give up. I would not take the easy path and 'manage.' Instead, I would continue to teach and train and research. This is a difficult choice. I read and write at 2am in the morning before a long day. But I can look colleagues in the eye—I can look our graduate students in the eye—as a highly published academic. The Springsteen-fuelled 'Glory Days' are not in the past. My best work is in the present. Research activity matters so much because it keeps leaders honest. Our work is checked by referees. We understand gatekeeping, its strengths and weaknesses, and we test ourselves in the field.

I want to be clear. It is incredibly tough running an academic career around a leadership role. But there is something powerful—liberating—enlivening—to not simply complain, but have the privilege to serve and reorient the language for leadership. I describe this model as leading from the back,[11] based on trust, integrity, respect and compassion. For women to enter these roles requires courage. We relinquish permanent posts. We lose financial security. We must be mobile. Further, middle management is the mincemeat of our universities: cheap, lacking structure and a bit bland without some spice. Still, each of us who have the privilege of working in a university can make a choice. We can complain about leadership and allow an orchard of bad apples to be appointed. Or, we can stand up. Take a risk. Fail. Be

---

[10] Fleming (2021).

[11] Brabazon (2020b).

overlooked. Backed into a glass cliff. The mediocrity and banality of the daily work functions are not pleasant. But leadership only improves when leaders do.

Joan Kirner and Moira Rayner realized that, "one of the greatest mistakes women can make is to assume that good intentions and hard work will be rewarded. They won't. You need power, to make a difference."[12] Women are rewarded within the patriarchy for performing traditional, disempowered feminine ideologies. Any movement outside of this narrow channel of femininity is critiqued, attacked and undermined. Jordan Peterson continues a long narrative of keeping women in a separate sphere from men and power. He attempts to render such hierarchies and distinctions both naturalized and validated.

> The people who hold that our culture is an oppressive patriarchy, they don't want to admit that the current hierarchy might be predicted on competence.[13]

Ignoring the tautological nature of his statement—here is the outcome that is justified because it is the outcome—there is also the difficult truth that the countervailing argument has more evidence. The current hierarchy is predicted on refusing women the right to education, refusing women the right to vote, refusing women the right to sit in parliament, refusing women the right to equal pay, and sustaining centuries of caring structures that means that the care for the young and the old defaults to women. This is also a discussion of leadership, and how the power differential is managed in workplaces as much as the family home. Leadership is not a checklist of attributes and characteristics. Leadership is relational. Men are in power because women are not. While leadership can be divisive, binarized and essentialist, newer models are emerging of transformative leadership. An effective proxy in ascertaining a feminist workplace is discovering women in positions of power, rather than a few isolated unicorns. Socially just leadership incorporates citizens of diverse ages, qualifications, ethnicity, races, genders and sexualities.

Jordan Peterson configures change as problematic. Change creates chaos. As he states,

> We don't know what women are like when they have political power because they've never had it. I mean, there's been queens, obviously, and that sort of thing … But this is a different thing and we don't know what a truly female political philosophy would be like.[14]

The assumption that vaginas create leadership styles, tropes and theories is amusing, if odd. But there are nations with different attitudes towards women, men and power. If scholars wish to explore a 'female political philosophy' and simultaneously recognize the errors and simplicity when deploying such a phrase, the nation of Aotearoa/New Zealand provides a strong case study. To date, Aotearoa/New Zealand has elected three female prime ministers, from the right and the left. All three have transcended the label of 'woman leader.' All three have battled complex financial and social conditions as the nation manages the ongoing challenges—and opportunities—of (post)colonialism. Jacinda Ardern, in her first term, had to manage a

---

[12] Kirner and Rayner (1999).

[13] Peterson and Bowles (2018).

[14] Peterson and Payne (2019).

terrorist event, involving the murder of New Zealanders during Friday prayers by an Alt-Right-affiliated white Australian, and a global pandemic. She also gave birth to her first child during this electoral cycle. Her goal was to bring compassion, listening, quick action and continual dialogue to the social and political fabric of Aotearoa/New Zealand. This is not a 'female political philosophy.' However, it is a demonstration of a feminist-framed commitment to decency, justice, law and transparency. Such commitments are available to all politicians, and all leaders, whether they possess ovaries or not.

Leadership, as Laura Hills realized, "is difficult to study."[15] But there is one truth. In its most relaxed, uncontested and natural form, it replicates nineteenth century colonial structures.[16] A white, heterosexual, procreative man is the most natural vessel into which leadership can be poured. Therefore, women are foreign, disconnected and unfamiliar when coveting leadership roles. The fit is unfamiliar. To describe patriarchy as ' a system' is too benevolent. It is a brutalizing, unjust and cruel mode of communication where the feminine is denied, discarded and disrespected at every turn.[17] Allowing business as usual—or water to find its own level—will not create change. The lack of space for women to be successful is well captured by the movement of clichés since the 1980s.

The glass ceiling has been replaced by the glass cliff. When women are granted leadership roles—often at a difficult time for an organization or in a housekeeping role to clean up a system, structure or strategy—these are referred to as 'glass cliff' roles.[18] They are fixed term positions, rendering the "manager-academic"[19] deeply unpopular because they are mopping up budgetary or structural issues, and do not progress to any other post or role. The only hope is to jump from glass cliff to

---

[15] Hills (2013).

[16] The absence in the discussion of colonization from Jordan Peterson's research career is startling considering he has lived most of his life in Canada, which is legally and socially negotiating and reconfiguring relationships between past injustices and present reconciliations. Instead, Peterson in *Beyond Order: 12 More rules for life*, (London: Penguin, 2021), celebrated a particular version of culture and history. He stated, "After I published my last book, my wife, Tammy, and I embarked on a lengthy speaking tour throughout the English-speaking world and a good part of Europe, particularly in the north. Most of the theaters I spoke at were old and beautiful, and it was a delight to be in buildings with such rich architectural and cultural histories, where so many of the bands we loved had played, and where other performing artists had had their great moments," p. 154. This odd 'celebration' of his personal success and its resonance with a particular version of 'cultural history' is significant, particularly considering the absence of colonial complexities in his research.

[17] Sara Ahmed described this process as, "the masculine idea of abstract moral autonomy structurally hinders members of subordinated groups from participating on a par with members of dominant groups in communicative interaction," from *Differences that matter: feminist theory and postmodernism*, (Cambridge: Cambridge University Press, 1998), p. 53.

[18] Brabazon and Schulz (2020).

[19] I note the power and problems in this unsettling hyphenated phrase. Please refer to R. Deem, "Gender, organizational cultures and the practices of manage academics in UK universities," *Gender, work and organization*, Vol 10, No. 2, 2003, pp. 239–259.

glass cliff posts, through precariat positions,[20] and attempt to gain stability.[21] These jumps—with hopes and promise and perhaps failure—commence with decisions that we make today and tomorrow. When a leadership moment appears for you dear reader, when you can choose to speak and question and reveal a vision, then grasp that moment. Every time we embody change, we enact it. We pivot rather than prop.

References

Adams, R. (2020, 27 February). Fewer than 1% of UK University Professors are black. The Guardian. https://www.theguardian.com/education/2020/feb/27/fewer-than-1-of-uk-university-professors-are-black-figures-show.

Aronowitz, S. (2000). *The Knowledge Factory*. Beacon.

Brabazon, T. (2020a). Leading from the back. *Realizing Leadership, 101,* 4–9. https://en.calameo.com/read/0060423302d540bd50322.

Brabazon, T. (2020b). From bad apples to zombies? Walking dead leadership in the contemporary university. *Fast Capitalism, 17*(2). https://fastcapitalism.journal.library.uta.edu/index.php/fastcapitalism/article/view/376/473.

Brabazon, T., & Schulz, S. (2020). Braving the bull: Women, mentoring and leadership in higher education. *Gender and Education, 32*(7), 873–890.

Fleming, P. (2021). *Dark academia: How universities die*. Pluto.

Hills, L. (2013). *Lasting female educational leadership: Leadership legacies of women leaders* (p. 17). Springer.

Kirner, J., & Rayner, M. (1999). *The women's power handbook* (p. 3). Penguin.

Larkins, F. (2011). *Australian higher education research policies and performance 1987–2010*. Melbourne University Press.

Peterson, J., & Paglia, C. (2017, 3 October). Modern Times with Camille Paglia and Jordan Peterson. *YouTube*. https://www.youtube.com/watch?v=v-hIVnmUdXM.

Peterson, J., & Bowles, N. (2018, 18, May). Custodian of the Patriarchy. *New York Times*. Jordan Peterson, Custodian of the Patriarchy - The New York Times (nytimes.com).

Peterson, J., & Payne, L. (2019). *A glitch in the matrix: Jordan Peterson and the Intellectual Dark Web*, p. 29. self-published.

Strachan, G. Broadbent, K., Whitehouse, G., Peetz, D., & Bailey, J. (2011, 4–7 July). Looking for Women in Australian Universities. In K. Krause, M. Buckridge, C. Grimmer, & S. Purbrick-Illek (Eds.) *Research and development in higher education: Reshaping higher education*, No. 34, pp. 308–319. Gold Coast, Australia.

Turner Kelly, B. (2019, 29 March). Though more women are on college campuses, climbing the professor ladder remains a challenge. Brookings.edu. https://www.brookings.edu/blog/brown-center-chalkboard/2019/03/29/though-more-women-are-on-college-campuses-climbing-the-professor-ladder-remains-a-challenge/.

---

[20] As Janelle Adsit, Sue Doe, Marisa Allison, Paula Maggio and Maria Maisto stated, "precarity is unevenly distributed in today's corporate university," from "Affective activism: answering institutional productions of precarity in the corporate university," *Feminist Formations*, Vol. 27, No 3, Winter 2015, pp. 21–48.

[21] The adjunct faculty is the archetype of this point. As Bryan Alexander confirmed, "adjunct faculty, who do more than anyone else, with less than anyone else … build the future of higher education," from *Academia Next: the future of higher education*, (John Hopkins University Press, 2020), loc 35.

Chapter 10
Rule 9–Teaching matters. Learning matters more

Jordan Peterson was not the first person to use social media and digitization to make money and build celebrity. Donald Trump did not invent misinformation online. The lack of information literacy—the capacity to read, assess, sort and sift—has been logged as a challenge in the online environment for well over a decade.

In January 2007, the Joint Information Systems Committee (JISC) published a report. It was titled, *Information behaviour of the researcher of the future*, and quickly became known as the Google Generation Report.[1] The research team tracked the reading behaviour of both students and teachers. The findings of the Report were startling and offered the clearest critique to glib phrases like the Google Generation, digital natives and digital immigrants.

1. All researchers—not only 'young people' - are skim reading research, reading abstracts rather than drilling deeper into a paper.
2. Young people are not 'dumbing down.' Society is 'dumbing down.'
3. "The information literacy of young people, has not improved with the widening access to technology."[2]
4. "Young scholars are using tools that require little skill: they appear satisfied with a very simple or basic form of searching."[3]
5. "Digital literacies and information literacies do not go hand in hand."[4]

The assumptions about digitization as efficient, productive and cheap formulated a university system where superficial learning, rapid degrees, and rubrics are the punctuation for undergraduate degrees.[5]

Richard Arum and Josipa Roksa's research in *Academically Adrift* has tracked the 'progress' of thousands of students through universities. Their results were startling.

---

[1] JISC (2007).

[2] ibid., p. 12.

[3] ibid., p.14.

[4] ibid., p. 20.

[5] To monitor the history and trajectory of online learning in universities, please refer to my trilogy: Brabazon (2002, 2007, 2013).

We found consistent evidence that many students were not being appropriately challenged. In a typical semester, 50% of students did not take a single course requiring more than 20 pages of writing, 32% did not have any classes that required reading more than 40 pages per week, and 36% reported studying alone five or fewer hours per week. Not surprisingly, given such a widespread lack of academic rigor, about a third of students failed to demonstrate significant gains in critical thinking, complex reasoning and writing ability during their four years of college.[6]

This situation was not caused by Twitter, YouTube, Facebook or Instagram. It has been triggered by a reduction in expectations for higher education. The fixation on speed and ease is now revealing long term consequences.[7]

Jordan Peterson has revealed this problem in situ. Ironically, considering his commentary on standards and the decline in universities through the presence of 'Marxists' teaching in humanities and arts faculties, his commitment to reading validates only a few sources and authors. To summon rigour and evidence requires reading widely, courageously and continually. Since 2013, well before C-16 and debates about trans rights, Peterson posted his lectures to YouTube.[8] In response to this proliferation of information, viewers see a stunning study, using unobtrusive research methods,[9] of banal lecturing, few references offered and basic ideas repeated to a classroom of students.[10] As with his public lectures, he does not use detailed notes. While this lack of notes is read by many of his followers as brilliance, his followers do not connect this lack of preparation with the dearth of references cited and the banality of the knowledge system he communicates.

In *12 rules* he states, "I cite Wikipedia because it is collectively written and edited and, therefore, the perfect place to find accepted wisdom."[11] To be clear, Wikipedia is where young men with time on their hands confuse the urgent and the important and the edgy and the significant. However, this is also a description of the Peterson audience. Peterson's videos receive a wide viewership of young men on YouTube,[12] with sizeable secondary audiences of White Supremacists, Evangelical Christians

---

[6] Arum and Roksa (2021).

[7] I note Benjamin Noys' statement, "speed is a problem. Our lives are too fast, we are subject to the accelerating demand that we innovate more, work more, enjoy more, produce more, and consume more, Noy (2014), p. x.

[8] What is significant is that Jordan Peterson uploaded material. He did record 'live' material for YouTube, but the majority of his materials were pre-recorded and uploaded, including his lectures. The digital delay in the presentation of this material is intriguing, explore how 'the present' is constructed and managed. The archive of YouTube is significant for Peterson, rather than the live delivery of content. For a discussion of 'live' media programming, please refer to Van Es (2017).

[9] Kellehear (2020), Knight (2018) and Lee (2000).

[10] Such simplistic and ahistorical distinctions are also located in his research. Please refer to Hirish et al. (2010).

[11] Peterson (2018).

[12] Bruce Riley Ashford stated that, "it is not surprising to find that Peterson is popular among conservative twentysomething males and other disaffected castaways of secular modernity." From "Jordan Person and the chaos of our secular age," in Dart (2020). Intriguing the critiques of 'post-modernism' move to 'secular modernity'. The greater question emerging from this statement is why these 'twentysomething males' are disaffected. One answer may be as social justice and strategies

and Paleoconservatives.[13] These are not fun people with whom to build and share a community. This is a dark, repressed, irrational space of xenophobia, narrow definitions of love, sex, desire and pleasure, and deep denials of any discussion of capitalism, the workplace, or the failures of the heteronormative, procreative family. The intrigue when assessing this community is that Jordan Peterson is - or, indeed, after his resignation, was - a university professor training clinical psychologists. Commonsensical life lessons about men, women, families and mothers are best left to morning television, private conversations or the pub. Instead, what is seen through these lecture videos is a university classroom, funded by taxpayers. The professionals he scaffolds through learning and teaching must assist very ill and troubled people. Such diagnostics and support are best delivered through the presentation of contemporary research, rather than talk more suited to the last two minutes of *Little House on the Prairie*. As Malik has confirmed, Peterson provides a "self-help manual for alienated men."[14] The clear argument and arc is that women are competing with men for education, jobs and life chances. If men seem to be losing in this 'war' of the sexes, then the result is grievance. How could a woman gain a high-quality degree? How did that woman gain that job? The default answer must be political correctness or prodiscrimination. The phrase 'political correctness' is a prophylactic to prevent men from recognizing that hard working women, who have sacrificed a great deal and overcome extraordinary barriers, have been successful. It is a way for an individual man to justify the conditions of his life. Political correctness—as a phrase—is a condom for consciousness.

I have personal experience with the Canadian University system and this issue is not isolated to a specific nation. I know that we are confronting challenges with standards throughout the world. I have moved through nine academic posts in my life, in four countries. I have managed that moment—that horrific moment—when the standards of the nation I have left   are not what I am seeing in a different nation. But then there is the Canadian story. I was Professor of Communication and I selected—as I always do—to teach first year students. The subject, predictably called Introduction to Communication, attracted a large group, not only filled with first year students majoring in the discipline, but a couple of hundred students who had enrolled in Communication as an 'easy' elective. Therefore, fourth year students were as common as first year students in my classroom. I wrote a tough and robust curriculum, with very challenging assessment. The first-year students only had the experience of me as a first-year lecturer, so they lifted to the required level. The fourth-year students struggled. They could not manage the weekly reading. The

---

to manage discrimination are enabled, 'twentysomething males' have their behaviours circumscribed. Intelligent women are applying for—and achieving—the employment opportunities that were outside the parameters of women before the widening participation agenda in universities. Groups must be confident in their power to give some of it away. Clearly, 'twentysomething men' are not confident in their power, or ability, to recognize that women worked hard and achieved results they did not. What makes this situation even more concerning is that these young men are reading Jordan Peterson describing the importance of competition in achieving life goals.

[13] Lynskey (2018).

[14] Malik (2019).

assignments required longer papers than they had been asked to write through their degree. When I came to aggregate the final marks in gradebook, I was stunned. Of the top twenty students, all were first year students. Not a single fourth year student received a mark in the ranked top twenty results for a first-year subject. For me, that was the moment where I saw Arum and Roksa's research coming to life. But after seeing Jordan Peterson's lectures, and the lack of content and rigour, and the incredibly slow delivery of very basic ideas, Arum and Roksa's argument was clearly visualized and I understood my experience with greater clarity.

I am not anti-lectures or lecturing. They can be passionate and powerful moments of learning. But the three Ds—digitization, disintermediation and deterritorialization—demand more of us as teachers and learners. Jordan Peterson was part of what Ray Land described as, "an inexorable shift in higher education away from this print-based culture to a digital culture."[15] Digital lectures should not replicate classroom-based instruction. Multimodality is probably the most important concept when considering contemporary education. Still, in 2013, Jordan Peterson recorded lectures he could have delivered in 1993 or 2003. The irony is that Jordan Peterson is questioning the value of a university education when his classroom is like a sub-Dr Phil. University education must be difficult. University lectures capture the best and most brilliant of scholars, inspiring the next generation of academics and professionals with powerful, modern theories and conflicting and engaging research. Lectures must be tough, difficult, complex and intricate. Most importantly, they are inspiring students to read and think, and read to think.

It is also significant to note that Peterson's methods for delivering material emerge from eight centuries of university history. Through most of the history of higher education, they were the locations for white, privileged men to improve themselves and become captains of industry, military leadership, run a government, or rule an empire. Leathwood and Hey confirmed that universities were configured as a site for white and privileged men to 'rationally' pursue knowledge.[16] Even now, as women are the majority of students in our universities, the disciplines in which women dominate are demeaned and undermined. STEM is - supposedly - the future. Health and education are the caring professions, underpaid and marginalized.

Before Peterson states (again) that it is time to remove the humanities from higher education, he may be advised to review international curricula and read the profound innovations in multimodality and Interface Studies. Jordan Peterson's lectures, which he has uploaded for our viewing and assessment, reveal the ontological complexity of a Disney movie. He holds no education qualifications. He has moved through teaching and research at elite universities. Then, many decades after the rest of us, he had to change or think about changing. His thinking about trans rights is only part of this story. It is a proxy. Actually, he needed to think about the diverse students in his classroom. Students are changing. Our andragogy must recognize this shift.

We teach what we need to learn. I have profound respect for all scholars and all disciplines. Teaching in universities is tough and it is my privilege to learn from

---

[15] Land et al. (2011).

[16] Leathwood and Hey (2009).

a community that chooses to make this task their life's work. But Jordan Peterson has continued to teach as he always had, riffing off headings. He taught the same course for years, used it as the foundation for his first scholarly monograph, and has generalized this teaching experience to other areas of his life. He is not a trained teacher and the research in "educational psychology" that has emerged to which he has attached his name is basic and simplistic,[17] disconnected from the intricate theories of teaching and learning that marinate our universities, particularly after the pandemic.

Young people look up to a lecturer and—if the andragogy is poorly constituted— may value very simple ideas on the basis of that respect. As Peterson's research area is clinical psychology, the overwhelming majority of papers are heavily co-authored. He is second and third author through most of his career, on most of his refereed scholarship. Peterson entered a particular mode of university teaching and did not move from it. He enacted a specific mode of empirical research and being an academic author. Addiction is an area of speciality.[18] However, he is a man, using academic credentials, to tell other men how to live and how to treat women.

He is not alone. Books like *The Coddling of the American Mind* argue that academics are blocking students from learning resilience using trigger warnings and cancel culture.[19] The problem is not cancel culture. The problem is a lack of information literacy. Are students fragile? Perhaps. The greater question is why students are fragile. Unemployment, under-employment, exorbitant fees for education, ridiculous payments for privatized utilities, and ill-informed public policies are only part of our corrosive present. Protests exist because there is no space to be different, to be defiant, and - in the case of George Floyd - to breathe. This is not emotion. This is not resentment or victimization. This is real. The challenge for scholars and citizens is how to manage nostalgia in education for a past that never existed. When university academics were older white men teaching younger white men, that system was scholarly and open. Now that the student and academic body are diverse in background and personal histories, these alternative information sources and narratives question what has been framed through university history as scholarly and open. New spaces of disagreement and learning have emerged. While the cascade of cliches about snowflakes and cancel culture proliferate, the more difficult work remains under addressed in considering how vulnerability is understood and mobilized.[20]

The person who should be head of all global Vice Chancellors is Professor Michael Roth, President of Wesleyan University. He confirmed the importance of what he described as 'safe enough spaces,' creating opportunities for different voices and views. Roth recognized that free speech is summoned whenever white middle-class people feel their rights being truncated. But he wants to avoid what he describes as the balkanization of universities through identity politics.[21] His project—that we should

---

[17] I note that Jordan Peterson is the third author of five in the Morisano et al. (2010).

[18] Peterson et al. (2005).

[19] Lukianoff and Haidt (2018).

[20] I note Koivunen et al. (2018).

[21] Roth (2019).

all consider—is how to create a space of disagreement and learning, remembering the role of education in democracy and overcoming oppression and poverty. Indeed, free speech is a permission slip for fear speech, summoning a false equivalence that all speech should be allowed. Further, free speech is not enforced listening. While the slogan 'no platform' is gaining traction, the point is that a person can speak, but they cannot order others to listen.

At its most basic, empowered citizens spend much energy moving attention away from the power that they hold. If attention is placed on why particular groups maintain authority over others, then scrutiny, accountability and evaluation would follow. To deflect such attention, anger is redirected to harpies, feminists, #blacklivesmatter activists, trans citizens, or university academics. As Owen Jones realized, "the real villains of the piece have not received anything like the attention they deserve."[22] Positions are protected. The power is protected. Freedom of speech is used to deflect and deny deep research, interpretation and public discussions about how and why power, money, prestige and authority is configured and distributed.

The summoning freedom of speech and the right to speak on all issues, regardless of the inexperience, incompetence or ignorance, meshes with a critique of "Postmodern NeoMarxism"[23] as hyper-relativist and creating a culture of equivalence in valuing of all views. In other words, it is freedom of speech for everyone with whom I agree, but with prohibited expression for the relativist "Postmodern NeoMarxists."[24] They do not have the right to speak or write, because of their commitment to relativism. This paradox remains unjustifiable. However strong questioning of this supposedly postmodern relativism emerged from the incisive scholar Richard Rorty. In 1982, he revealed that this configuration of postmodernism and relativism is not only wrong, but ridiculous.

> Relativism is the view that every belief on a certain topic, or perhaps about any topic, is as good as every other. No one holds this view. Except for the occasional cooperative freshman, one cannot find anybody who says that two incompatible opinions on an important topic are equally good.[25]

Homology in teaching and learning is always matched by nostalgia. When we were taught by white men, our universities were seen to be rigorous, excellent and maintaining high standards. Now that it may be a bit uncomfortable to talk about racism or colonization as a white man with students of colour in the room, or to probe the pay differential between men and women in a classroom dominated by women, or citizenship rights when trans or non binary identifying students are in a lecture theatre with many entitlements for employment not yet secure, the focus is on how freedom of speech for these white men is inhibited. They are unnerved that the truths they have taught for generations no longer maintain the audience or currency. Our task is to recognize that some members of our university community are fragile, and

---

[22] Jones (2015).

[23] Peterson (2017).

[24] ibid.

[25] Rorty (1982).

that fragility is understandable. It is not to be greeted with words like snowflake, or mantras like 'toughen up princess.' Instead, the project of the university transforms. We must explore how we can maintain standards without standardization.

References

Arum, R., & Roksa, J. (2011). College, too easy for its own good. *Los Angeles Times*. Retrieved June 2, 2011, from http://www.latimes.com/news/opinion/commentary/la-oe-arum-college-201 10602,0,1981136.story.

Brabazon, T. (2002). *Digital Hemlock: Internet education and the poisoning of teaching*. UNSW Press.

Brabazon, T. (2007). *The University of Google*. Ashgate.

Brabazon, T. (2013). *Digital dieting: From information obesity to digital fitness*. Ashgate.

Dart, R. (2020). *Myth and meaning in Jordan Peterson: A Christian perspective* (p. 24). Lexham Press.

Hirsh, J. B., DeYoung, C. G., Xu, X., & Peterson, J. B. (2010). Compassionate liberals and polite conservative: associations of agreeableness with political ideology and moral values. *Personality and Social Psychology Bulletin, 36*(5), 655–664.

JISC. (2007). Information behaviour of the researcher of the future. In: CIBER briefing paper. UCL, London. http://www.jisc.ac.uk/media/documents/programmes/reppres/gg_final_ keynote_11012008.pdf.

Jones, O. (2015). *The establishment: And how they get away with it* (p. xi). Penguin.

Kellehear, A. (2020). *The unobtrusive researcher: A guide to methods*. Routledge.

Knight, A. (2018). Innovations in unobtrusive methods. In: Byman, A., & Buckanan, D (Eds.) *Unconventional methodology in organization and management research*. Oxford University Press, Oxford, pp 64–83.

Koivunen, A., Kyrola, K., & Ryberg, I. (2018). *The power of vulnerability: Mobilising affect in feminist, queer and anti-racist media culture*. Manchester University Press.

Land, R., Land, R., Bayne, S. (Eds). *Digital Difference: Perspectives on online learning*. Sense Publishers, p. 62.

Leathwood, C., & Hey, V. (2009). Gender/ed discourses and emotional sub-texts: Theorising emotion in UK higher education. *Teaching in Higher Education, 14*(4), 429–440.

Lee, R. (2000). *Unobtrusive methods in social research*. Open University Press.

Lukiannoff, G., & Haidt, J. (2018). *The coddling of the American Mind: How good intentions and bad ideas are setting up a generation for failure*. Penguin.

Lynskey, D. (2018). How dangerous is Jordan B Peterson, the right-wing professor who 'hit a hornets' nest'?. *The Guardian*. February 8, 2018. https://www.theguardian.com/science/2018/ feb/07/how-dangerous-is-jordan-b-peterson-the-rightwing-professor-who-hit-a-hornets-nest.

Malik, N. (2019). *We need new stories: Challenging the toxic myths behind our age of discontent* (p. 15). Weidenfeld and Nicolson.

Morisano, D., Hirsh, J. B., Peterson, J., Pihl, R., & Shore, B. (2010). Setting, elaborating, and reflecting on personal goals improves academic performance. *Journal of Applied Psychology, 95*(2), 255.

Noys, B. (2014). *Accelerationism and capitalism* (p. x). Zero Books.

Peterson, J. (2018). *12 Rules for Life: An antidote for chaos* (p. 114). Penguin.

Peterson, J., Morey, J., & Higgins, D. (2005). You drink, I drink: Alcohol consumption, social context and personality. *Individual Differences Research, 3*, 23–35.

Peterson, J. (2017). Postmodern Neomarxism: diagnosis and cure, Jordan B Peterson. *YouTube*. July 10, 2017. https://www.youtube.com/watch?v=s4c-jOdPTN8

Rorty, R. (1982). *Consequences of pragmatism*. University of Minnesota Press.

Roth, M. (2019). *Safe enough spaces: A pragmatist's approach to inclusion, free speech, and political correctness on college campuses* (p. 43). Yale University Press.
Van Es, K. (2017). *The future of live*. Polity.

Chapter 11
Rule 10–Woman are humans, citizens and fully formed people

My goal in this rule is not troll inversion, to shame or to mock or to crush anyone including Jordan Peterson. The goal is not to be cruel. To shame.[1] Watching Jordan Peterson's videos, I rarely felt anger. My most common response was despair. It was a despair summoned from the realization that a human being could discount the lives, complexity, hopes and capacities of women with such carelessness. Trans communities were denied the right to name, claim and situate themselves in safety and in space. These denials are aligned.

Jordan Peterson reveals many errors in his engagements with women. Firstly, he conflates radical feminism with all feminism.[2] Feminism has a history, and it is complex, powerful and diverse. He offers very simple renderings of the patriarchy. He repeats 'natural' hierarchies to demonstrate why there are gender differences. Yes—the lobsters are the archetype of this argument. He creates male victims to decentre and erase women's issues. For Peterson, feminism prevents men from being men and allows women to dominate universities and the workplace. Because of this domination, men move to Alt-Right organizations. This is the intellectual equivalent of men going to their shed to avoid the nagging woman asking them to take out the garbage.

Peterson's presentation of girls and women for his male audience in *12 Rules* is pathetic. It is also concerning, oppressive, intellectually inelegant and ahistorical.

> Girls can win by winning in their own hierarchy—by being good at what girls' value, as girls.[3]

> The increasingly short supply of university-educated men poses a problem of increasing severity for women who want to marry, as well as date.[4]

---

[1] I recognize Peter Stearns and his powerful book *Shame: A brief history*, (Urbana: University of Illinois Press, 2017).

[2] M. Trejo, "On Peterson's Anti-feminism," from B. Burgis et al. (2020).

[3] Peterson (2018).

[4] ibid., p. 300.

© The Author(s), under exclusive license to Springer Nature Singapore Pte Ltd. 2022
T. Brabazon, *12 Rules for (Academic) Life*,
https://doi.org/10.1007/978-981-16-9291-8_11

Those of us who have been a part of this patriarchal rodeo in the past remember Susan Faludi's fine work in *Stiffed*.[5] She demonstrated how such statements are used to agitate women to think if 'we' are smart, then men will not like us. If women hold a degree, then they may not be even dateable. Dating a mediocre bloke has never been a life goal of momentum and power. Feminism provides women with choices beyond marrying a man that wants to crow his importance to a supportive, suppliant date. The imperative of being a feminist is to recognize and affirm women's journey from experience to expertise, life to consciousness. Men's journey from experience to expertise, from life to consciousness, requires new skills including the capacity to listen and learn from emerging spaces, literacies, lives and narratives of trans, intersex, and non-binary identifying citizens. These will not always be comfortable conversations because our culture values heterosexual men talking with other heterosexual men, and often about people who are not heterosexual men. But if learning, listening and literacies entwine, new conversations, narratives and patterns of ideas emerge. These conversations begin with listening. They move to understanding and literacy, and—hopefully—configure a more socially just and intricate political landscape, to enable change. It is important to return to the history of feminism and remember why we needed that Virginia Woolf-inspired room of our own.

Peterson affirmed the value of separate spheres—the masculine order and feminine chaos. Such a societal configuration also reinforces and justifies Christianity and the market economy. Women are controlled and managed by being married, having children, running a household and accepting less. If this narrative is not followed, then men's 'self-reliance'—so validated in popular cultural genres from Westerns to Science Fiction—is questioned. Men's suffering—for Peterson—is the price that 'society' pays when women do not follow the bouncing ball of the patriarchal tune.[6] What I summon in this Rule—and this book more generally—is a desire that women be accepted as fully human. We speak with our mouths, not our vaginas. We think with intelligence, not through our ovaries. We are complex, diverse and thoughtful, rich in spirit, and bold in action. To ignore such truths allows men to live comfortable lives where their needs, hopes, ambitions and decisions are centralized. Women have lived a life of marginalization, decentring, of never being enough, because we are not a man. Our task is to find and occupy that room of our own, but then create space and silence for new movements, communities and communication systems.

I am a white, heterosexual feminist. I have had the privilege of being very highly educated and working in our university sector. My role is not to speak on the behalf of feminists of colour, men, masculinity scholars and men's studies scholars, the trans community, non-binary identifying colleagues and positions or affinities and tendencies on the continuum of life that we do not have the language to describe or understand. I do not share those experiences. I listen. I read. I research. I cite.

[5] Faludi (1999).

[6] Neuroscience can be involved in the configuration of this 'pink' and 'blue' brain. Gina Rippon is her book *The Gendered Brain*, (London: Penguin, 2020) analysed the studies confirming different brains and showed the profound errors in their methods. She described them as "neurotrash.".

I change. I think. But unlike Chaka Khan, I am not every woman.[7] I am a woman born and living at the edge of the world. I stand as a scholar and as a woman, having lived the contradictions between those two nouns, and with a goal to ensure they mesh for the generations of scholarly women that follow. Feminism is not a singular movement. It maintains complex relationships with other progressivists movements. It offers the language to pivot, to pause, to think, to reflect, to hope and to challenge.

Our task is to connect me to we. A question that has worried me throughout my non-working life, is how politically effective is identity politics? How exactly does the Gay and Lesbian Mardi Gras change the way we think about family, sex and identity? How does the Black Lives Matter movement change the prejudices that white citizens articulate every day? Does feminism work anymore? If it does, then why are so many women reticent to claim the word? These are not rhetorical questions. They require honest research to present transparent and complex answers.

This is confronting and difficult scholarship. Forces on the left and right use terms like identity politics. This phrase shuts down debates and discussion. We assume that identity politics has always existed. It has not. In an *Encyclopedia of the Social Sciences*, published in 1968, there was no entry under identity.[8] Thinking about identity is a very new intellectual and social enterprise. The impact of the women's movement, gay movement and the multicultural/melting pot ideology in the United States has had an impact. Concrete political advances have been made by identity groups. But there are problems.

Hobsbawm stated in *The Age of Extremes*, "never was the word 'community' used more indiscriminately and emptily than in the decade when communities in the sociological sense became hard to find in real life."[9] Identity politics has a paradox at its core: men and women choose to belong to an identity group, but the choice is based on the belief that they have no choice but to belong to the othered community or group. There is so much talk about outsiders that insiders are left off the hook. If there were no outsiders, then the insiders would have to face up to their responsibilities.

Identity is context specific. It is transitory. Political movements, with goals, infrastructure and long-term projects and commitments, cannot be based on ephemeral identity commitments. The mass political movements of the Left were coalition or group alliances that were held together by universal causes from the 1880s right through to the First World War. The left could not be based on mass labour parties because the working class in most countries was small. Since the 1970s, the Left has been seen as a coalition of minority groups. The problematic articulation of the left and the nation has resulted in the forces of the right claiming the national popular, claiming the rhetorical ground and speaking for the entire nation. Consider Donald Trump and 'Make America Great Again.' This mode of slogan demonstrates and confirms this change in the political shaping of nationalism. It was not always the case. At the end of WW2, the Left everywhere in Europe represented the nation, because the nation had represented resistance during the war. It had been the left that

---

[7] Khan (2020).

[8] Hobsbawm (1996).

[9] Hobsbawm (1994).

had fought fascism. This fight against the forces on the right generated a commonality between citizens that transgressed classes, nations, age and genders and also gave the working-class bargaining power. There was a solid and effective match between patriotism and leftist social transformation at the end of the Second World War.

This desire for change ended soon after 1945. By 1951, every ideology in Europe had been exhausted, liberalism by the first world war, conservatism by the appeasement process before World War Two, fascism by the Second World War, and the left by the post-war reconstruction. It was the Conservatives who were first able to re-establish consensus. Except on a few occasions in the 1960s, the left has had to react and respond to the political forces around them. It was Thatcher and Reagan who changed the rules of the game. New sites for political contestation, new social antagonisms, new social movements and new political identities emerged. There was a repositioning of tradition, family and nation.[10] Thatcher and Reagan created a new national popular culture because the left had failed to develop a coherent policy that had credibility and national significance. Without the New Right of Thatcher and Reagan, identity politics would not have emerged.

There was a loss in this political struggle. By decentring economics and dissociating the economic and the cultural, we now have race and gender as the new base. Culture becomes an expression or articulation of these societal structures. The current rendering of this debate includes phrases like 'cancel culture' or 'toxic masculinity.' There remains remarkable research in men's studies and masculinity studies that has and continues to produce powerful theorizing of men—by men. Jeff Hearn[11] remains an incredible scholar of masculinity, as does Michael Kimmel.[12] A more recent intervention is from Andrew Manno. His book on *Toxic masculinity*

---

[10] I note Dawne McCance's outstanding research into Derrida's seminar series, delivered at the Ecole Normale Superieur in the 1975–6 academic year. She explores how Derrida probed the way in which traditions were received, and then filtered and restructured. Please refer to D. McCance (2019).

[11] To view a selection of Jeff Hearn's monographs on men and masculinity, please refer to: *Men in the public eye: the construction and deconstruction of public men and public patriarchies*, (London: Routledge, 1992), *The violence of Men: how men talk about and how agencies respond to men's violence to women*, (London: Routledge, 1998), *Men and masculinities in Europe*, (London: Whiting and Birch, 2006), *Sex, violence and the body: the erotics of wounding*, (Houndmills: Palgrave, 2008), and *Men of the world: genders, globalizations, transnational times*, (London: SAGE, 2015).

[12] For example, please refer to Michael Kimmel's remarkable scholarly monographs: *Men Confront Pornography*, (New York, Crown, 1991), *Against the tide: pro-feminist men in the U.S., 1776–1990*, (Boston: Beacon Press, 1992), *The politics of manhood*, (Philadelphia: Temple University Press, 1995), *Changing Men: new directions in the study of men and masculinity*, (Newbury Park, SAGE, 1996), *The gender of desire: essays on masculinity*, (Albany: State University of New York Press, 2005), *Guyland: the perilous world where boys become men*, (New York: Harper, 2008), *Misframing men: the politics of contemporary masculinities*, (New Brunswick: Rutgers University Press, 2010), *Men's Lives*, (Boston: Allyn and Bacon, 2010), *The gendered society*, (New York: Oxford University Press, 2011), *Manhood in America: a cultural history*, (New York: Oxford University Press, 2012), *Angry white men: American masculinity at the end of an era*, (New York: Nation Books, 2013). I have presented this selection of Professor Kimmel's research career to demonstrate that powerful scholars have explored masculinity, with subtly, care and precision, since the 1980s. Professor Peterson's commentaries on boys and men do not cite this powerful research from Men's Studies and

and casino capitalism demonstrated the consequences of a winner take all hyper capitalism.[13] Manno reveals the stories available for men as post-industrial workers and they invoke toughness, independence and aggression. The online radicalization of young men often starts with racism and sexism but concludes with a sense of entitlement and loss of privilege.[14]

The Alt-Right matters to these debates and this historical moment because they have disconnected from traditional conservatism, by clustering economic freedom and the reduction in state power, national defence and traditional morality. Jordan Peterson matters to this political cluster, being described by Tabatha Southey as "a belle of the Alt-Right."[15] His status as an academic and researcher verified the subjective, the oppressive and the discriminatory. The Alt-Right deploys attacks on women as the gateway drug into this ideology. Men who cannot seem to 'get' a woman or 'hold' a woman are easy to target in their dissatisfaction. From this gateway culture of blaming women for the failures of men, the attacks move—predictably— to migrants and citizens of colour. The shift in emphasis is to affirm the greatness of white people and white history, justifying the distribution of resources, power and privilege. It is like *Mad Max* meets a zombie movie. Behind the smoke and mirrors—and blame cultures—are real problems to address.

White working-class men no longer in work are angry,[16] and that is legitimate anger. Blaming women or a particular faith structure or skin colour for that injustice is not real, viable or accurate. This is why Jordan Peterson was needed by the Alt-Right. He loaned academic credibility to this blame culture as he stressed the value and benefit of the current hierarchies and spheres for men and women. To cite Peterson, "Violent attacks are what happens when men do not have partners, and society needs to work to make sure those men are married."[17] Note the inevitability of Peterson's narrative. Violence 'happens' if women decide that heteronormative partnering is not in their interests. Women have to behave in ways that are not in their interests because 'society' is in danger from violent men who cannot control themselves. Women become the social prophylactic, the vaccine to violence. Or—put another way— women are *Damned Whores and God's Police*,[18] protecting men from themselves and other women.

This is not a metaphoric threat, although Peterson's own research confirmed that a "metaphoric threat is more real than real threat."[19] Zygmunt Bauman once stated that, "One thinks of identity whenever one is not sure where one belongs."[20] Now

---

Masculinity Studies. To wilfully ignore such research is not only anti-intellectual, but demonstrates that his views are not based in or derived from the refereed literature in this field.

[13] Manno (2020).

[14] ibid., p. 49–50.

[15] Southey (2017).

[16] Hochschild (2016).

[17] Peterson in Bowles (2018).

[18] Summers (1975).

[19] Peterson and DeYoung (2000).

[20] Bauman (1996).

with the Alt-Right, the identity politics that dares not speak its name emerging from straight, white men. We have wars over identity and belonging. These discussions are unstable and volatile, because we have relinquished the conversations about the economy. The Global Financial Crisis happened. Neoliberalism destroyed economic and social systems through a lack of regulation.[21] Yet we are here—over a decade later—talking about identity.[22]

Black lives matter. Me too matters. Trans lives matter. None of these truths are arbitrary, unfair or unreasonable. Indeed, they are crucial to transformative change. The tougher question is why identity is a self-contained entity, unconnected to the economic scaffold. Remember Bauman statement once more: "One thinks of identity whenever one is not sure where one belongs."[23] Where do you belong? Following on from Hobsbawm—how do we build the connections that transcend identity and builds the coalition—the bridge—to others with the goal of resetting conversations about our economic lives?

Jordan Peterson has perpetuated the identity politics that he critiqued. He created an identity for young, white men, reversed victim ideologies and rendered them the victim of feminists, postmodernists and Marxists. Because identity is not connected to economics, irrational inversions and false equivalences such as these can be made. Trans rights can be denied to reclaim the rights of heterosexual white men. White men's speech is free speech. Anything else is compelled speech. There are opportunities to refashion this political landscape. In moving from me to we, connections are created, and new realities summoned.

References

Bauman, Z. (1996). From pilgrim to tourist. In S. Hall & P. du Gay (Eds.), *Questions of Cultural Identity*, p. 19. London: SAGE.

Bowles, N. (2018, 18 May). Jordan Peterson, Custodian of the Patriarchy. *The New York Times.* https://www.nytimes.com/2018/05/18/style/jordan-peterson-12-rules-for-life.html.

Burgis, B., Hamilton, C., McManus, M., & Trejo, M. (2020). *Myth and Mayhem: A leftist critique of Jordan Peterson* (p. 197). Zero Books.

Faludi, S. (1999). *Stiffed*. Chatto and Windus.

---

[21] Gillian Tett used the evocative phrase, "dancing around the regulators," from *Fool's Gold: how unrestrained greed corrupted a dream, shattered global markets and unleashed a catastrophe,* (London: Little Brown, 2009), p. 26.

[22] Speed and digitization are important forces in understanding the GFC. Paul Virilio stated that, "the economic crash that we experienced in 2007–2008 was a systemic crash with a history, a history going back to the early 1980s when a global stock exchange was first connected in real time. This connection, called 'Program Trading,' also had another highly suggestive name: the Big Band of the markets. A first crash in 1987 confirmed and concretised the impossibility of managing this speed. The crash in 2008, which was partly caused by 'flash trading,' or very fast computerised listings done on the same computers as those used in national defence … Our reality has become uninhabitable in milliseconds, picoseconds, femtoseconds, billionths of seconds," from P. Virilio (2021).

[23] Bauman, *op. cit.*

Hobsbawm, E. (1996, May/June). Identity politics and the left. *New Left Review* (217), 38.

Hobsbawm, E. (1994). *The age of extremes* (p. 428). Vintage.

Hochschild, A. R. (2016). *Strangers in their own land: Anger and mourning on the American right.* The New Press.

Khan, C. (2020). I'm every woman. *Rhino YouTube Channel.* https://www.youtube.com/watch?v= DVDCNmdi7QI. Manno, A. (2020). *Toxic masculinity, casino capitalism, and America's favorite card game: The poker mindset.* Cham: Springer.

McCance, D. (2019). *The reproduction of Life Death: Derrida's La vie la mort.* Fordham University Press.

Manno, A. (2020). Toxic masculinity, casino capitalism, and America's favorite card game: The poker mindset. Cham: Springer.

Peterson, J. (2018). *12 Rules for Life: An antidote for chaos* (p. 298). Penguin.

Peterson, J., & DeYoung, C. (2000). Metaphoric threat is more real than real threat. *Behavioral and Brain Sciences, 23*(6), 214–215.

Southey, T. (2017, 17 November). Is Jordan Peterson the stupid man's smart person? *Maclean's.* Is Jordan Peterson the stupid man's smart person?—Macleans.ca.

Summers, A. (1975). *Damned Whores and God's Police: The Colonization of Women in Australia.* Melbourne: Allen Lane.

Virilio, P. (2021). *The administration of fear*, pp. 34–35. Los Angeles: Semiotexte.

Chapter 12
Rule 11–Respect the vulnerable, the sick, the dying and the dead

Jordan Peterson talks a great deal about individualism, strength and suffering, but very little about respect, particularly respect for the sick, the dying and the dead. Let me explain. I have not entered the Peterson debates since 2016 for many reasons. I did not wish to validate the mediocre. But it was the Post Peterson paradigm, after the debate with Zizek in April 2019 and the personal issues that were rendered public and political, that moved me to action. I realized I am one of the few academics—feminist academics—that can speak these words from truth, rather than hypocrisy.

I offer these words to call out the hypocrisy of a man who tells other men how to live up to their responsibilities. When his moment came to be tested, he failed. My intervention is not only about one man and his failure to be the person he was instructing others to be. I log this issue, not as a matter of an individual's strength, weakness or choices, but as a reminder to value decency and respect, even at the end.

We are judged as an individual, but also as a community and a culture, for how we treat the young, the old, the vulnerable, the sick and the dying. We are not lobsters grasping terrain, snapping off the legs of the weak. It remains a privilege of the empowered to walk away from the sickness and death of others. Hypocrisy is a malignant growth in intellectual and political life. We are used to members of conservative parties sprouting heteronormative family values, while running mistresses, lies and denials. We have seen the clergy sermonize on celibacy while exploiting the young people in their care.

Jordan Peterson talked a great deal about individual men and their responsibilities, but his failures to be a man, with all the imponderable mash up of contradictory and silent ideologies that marinate that noun, have been starkly revealed. That he did not assume responsibility through his wife's cancer and recovery is an ugly truth, but one that must be brought into the light. It must be discussed and recognized. Jordan Peterson stated that, "the purpose of life is finding the largest burden that you can bear and bearing it."[1] Jordan Peterson failed by his own criterion of life's purpose, and this failure has consequences.

---

[1] Peterson (2018a).

© The Author(s), under exclusive license to Springer Nature Singapore Pte Ltd. 2022
T. Brabazon, *12 Rules for (Academic) Life*,
https://doi.org/10.1007/978-981-16-9291-8_12

Tammy Peterson was diagnosed with cancer in early 2019. It was confirmed as kidney cancer and severe in February 2019. Two surgeries were conducted, the second of which damaged her lymphatic system. She has survived what was described as a terminal illness. Yet her views, desires or wishes for the degree of publicity or privacy granted to this illness are not known. Her husband, Jordan Peterson, went public with her illness and then—with even more publicity—demonstrated his inability to manage it. Although having what he described as "a lot of help"[2] and a job where he could be away on sick leave for extended months, Peterson started taking anti-anxiety medication and became addicted to prescription drugs by August 2019.[3] He entered a series of rehabilitation centres in the United States, Russia and Serbia.

This story is strange enough until we enter YouTube, the playground of the weird, inflammatory and self-absorbed. For July 11, 2020's "Peterson family update" delivered from Serbia, Jordan Peterson talks with his daughter for nearly an hour.[4] This is a horrific, train wreck hour, transcending even Prince Andrew's interview where he denied having sex with young women and sweating, probably in that order.[5] Peterson spent the hour showing that when a spouse is sick, a man's best strategy is to focus on himself. Tammy Peterson's illness became a prop to continue his publicity,[6] and maintain his celebrity, after the loss of his profile through his performance in the Zizek debate. Jordan Peterson stated that while managing his addiction to prescription drugs, he had not been with his wife beyond a few days between December 2019 and July 2020.[7]

What viewers see in this video is banality, low level vocabulary, profound self-absorption, a pathetic garnering for sympathy and a fully flowered 'poor me' narrative. He also talked about a new book, which became another instalment of *12 Rules*, released in March 2021.[8] He could not be with his sick wife, but he could write his third book. In this hour-long interview, his wife and her illness were de-emphasized. Instead, he expressed how unpleasant this illness was for him personally. All the events of 2020—Australian bushfires, Covid-19, economic recession, the climate emergency, #blacklivesmatter, sustainability[9]—none of these events are

---

[2] "Peterson Family Update," YouTube, July 11, 2020, https://www.youtube.com/watch?v=GzR bEMzr0k8.

[3] It is significant to note his research in this area. Please refer to Peterson et al. (2003).

[4] "Peterson Family Update," *op. cit.*

[5] Prince Andrew & the Epstein Scandal: The Newsnight Interview - BBC News, *BBC YouTube Channel*, November 17, 2019, https://www.youtube.com/watch?v=QtBS8COhhhM.

[6] Intriguingly, one of the few commentaries Tammy Peterson offered about her experiences on her own terms was in 2021, the month of Jordan Peterson's release of his third monograph. She was interviewed in "A Conversation on Personal Growth with Tammy Peterson," YouTube, January 26, 2021, https://www.youtube.com/watch?v=1-dD3UwwShQ from Kintore College. The first question of this interview asked her about the illness and how prayer helped her overcome it. However, what is important about this interview is that Tammy Peterson expressed her narrative in her own way. What is also significant is the absence of Jordan Peterson's support from her narrative.

[7] ibid.

[8] Peterson (2021).

[9] Cook (2019).

even mentioned in the hour-long interview. The focus was himself and his addiction. When *Beyond Order: 12 More Rules for Life* emerged in March 2021, this lack of engagement with the global tragedies, sickness, grief, illness and injustice was explained with the stylistic flick of a hand. Peterson made a decision "to concentrate on addressing issues not specific to the current time."[10] This is a decision of the powerful to dismiss a pandemic and focus on other 'issues.' A denial of the present is a denial of reality, a reorganization of the world like a chess game without rules.

Significantly, in his 2021 self-help book, those 'other issues' involved a long passage explaining his illness and how he responded to his wife's sickness. Once more, he was the victim. His wife "recovered rapidly and, to all appearances, completely—a testament to the luck without which none of us can live, and her own admirable strength and resistance."[11] For a supposed scientist to confirm that luck, strength and resistance 'cured' a supposedly terminal disease is dangerous and disingenuous. However, this narrative needed to be constructed in *Beyond Order: 12 More Rules for Life* so that the readers could move to the main event: Jordan Peterson's drug abuse and recovery. Taking anti-anxiety drugs from 2017, this medicalization was justified, not through the illness of his wife, but through his success.

> I continued the benzodiazepine for almost exactly three years, because my life did seem unnaturally stressful during that time (the period when my life changed from the quiet existence of a university professor and clinician to the tumultuous reality of a public figure).[12]

The story becomes Peterson's battle with drug abuse. He states, "I was plagued, for my part, with the likely loss of someone."[13] Yet at the point where he was needed to care and assist his family, his 'illness' of addiction resulted in months away from a sick wife. His needs were the priority.

Such a decision is convenient for those in power. What COVID-19 has taught us is that neglecting the public—public education, public good, public health—will kill people.[14] Focusing on individual choices and individual rights will kill people. When asked by Peterson's daughter how his followers are meant to feel about his addiction and inability to manage his wife's illness, he stated, "If you're going to wait to learn from people who don't make mistakes or don't have tragedy enter their life, you're going to spend a long time waiting to learn something."[15] In the comments section of YouTube, his followers quoted this line like the *Life of Brian*.[16] You are all individuals. Yes. We are all individuals. As Joseph Reagle confirmed, "in sifting through the comments, we can learn much about ourselves and the way that other

---

[10] Peterson, *Beyond Order: 12 More rules for life*, op. cit., xiii.

[11] ibid., xvi.

[12] ibid., xvi.

[13] ibid., xxi.

[14] I note Naomi Klein's convincing argument in *No is not enough: defeating the new shock politics*, (London: Allen Lane, 2017). She probes the relationship between neoliberalism and the public sphere. She states, "neoliberalism is shorthand for an economic project that vilifies the public sphere," p. 79.

[15] "Peterson Family Update," *op. cit.*

[16] *Life of Brian*, (Handmade Films, 1979).

people seek to explore the value of our social selves."[17] These comments reveal that an academic presenting clear 'rules' for how to live and then not meeting his own standards can be reoriented and reconfigured with populist punctuation.

This is a man whose wife became sick and he could not manage it, and became hooked on prescription drugs. That is bad enough. It is made worse when researchers remember that he completed his graduate work on—you are ahead of me, dear reader—addiction.[18] What are those young men meant to learn about this story of a man who could not manage anxiety when his wife needed him? Life presented Jordan Peterson with a test and he failed it. The importance of "bearing witness"[19] to the sickness and, perhaps, death of an intimate partner is difficult, debilitating work. It holds no purpose but to value and validate a life lived, a love shared, and a micro-moment of dignity and clarity at the shared suffering and loss of a person and a future. There is no life-saving product, hope or outcome. The singular aim is to create a meaningful ending for a person who has lost everything.

The narrative arc presented in this Rule is not an individual matter. The research shows that Jordan Peterson is just like so many other men when confronted by the illness of their partner. The Peterson case highlights the incredibly high rate of men leaving their wives when they become sick.[20] Researching patients from the Seattle Cancer Care Alliance, Huntsman, and Stanford University School of Medicine, a study was published with profound results. Titled "Men leave: separation and divorce far more common when the wife is the patient,"[21] the research confirmed that women were six times more likely to be separated or divorced soon after diagnosis of cancer or multiple sclerosis than if the man in the relationship is a patient. This is termed "partner abandonment."[22] This study confirms that the one meaningful research variable in monitoring partner abandonment is gender. The women that are abandoned have a poorer recovery rate than other women. This cascade of injustice

---

[17] Reagle (2015).

[18] Jordan Peterson's PhD was titled "Potential Psychological markers for the predisposition to alcoholism," McGill University, 1990, https://escholarship.mcgill.ca/concern/theses/7d278v86c. Examples of the later research emerging from this thesis include R. Pihl and J. Peterson, "Drugs and aggression: correlations, crime and human manipulative studies and some proposed mechanisms," *Journal of Psychiatry and Neuroscience*, Vol. 20, No. 2, 1995, p. 141.

[19] Fisher (2019).

[20] Significantly, Jordan Peterson in *Beyond Order: 12 More rules for life*, (London: Penguin, 2021) confirmed his surprise at men who can manage the sickness of their wives. For example, in Rule 3, Peterson writes about his father-in-law Dell Roberts and his care for his wife Beth who had dementia. This caring role was discussed in the following terms: "I love my father-in-law. I respect him, too. He is extremely stable emotionally – one of those tough or fortunate people (perhaps a little of both) who can let the trials and tribulations of life roll off him and keep moving forward with little complaint and plenty of competence … When his wife, Beth, now deceased, developed dementia at a relatively young age, he took care of her in an uncomplaining and unresentful a manner as anyone could imagine. It was impressive. I am by no means convinced that I could have fared as well," p. 87. What Jordan Peterson does not seem to recognize is that he did not fare as well. He was given the opportunity to place the care of his wife at the centre of his responsibilities.

[21] Glantz et al. (2009).

[22] ibid.

and inequality moves to even more debilitating terrain: the older the woman, the more likely the relationship as to end.[23]

Similarly, a study of brain cancer in 2009 again demonstrated that the strongest predictor of separation or divorce was whether or not the sick person was a woman. In this research, men were seven times more likely to leave their partner than the other way around. These studies demonstrate—from the last two decades and when using control groups—that serious illnesses in wives make husbands more likely to leave. Serious illnesses in husbands make wives more likely to stay.

It gets worse. In March 2020 when Poppy Noor presented an investigative journalism piece in *The Guardian*, she showed that when women become sick, expectations remain intact for the continuation of paid work and housework by their partners.[24] If men do stay, then they will not help with the housework while women recover or—indeed—die. This is dreadful research to present, and this is why Jordan Peterson's behaviour is so damning for the young men who follow him. Yes, he is a hypocrite, but he is behaving just like so many other men. Women's illnesses become an inconvenience, a moment of spotlight depravation for men, a fear of abandonment.

This situation is why I punch these brutalizing words onto a screen, and they tumble to the page. I ask more of men, and I ask that heterosexual men treat their partners with respect. Once more, let us rehearse the rhetoric. I am not describing all men. But more men abandon their sick wives than women abandon their sick husbands. I am reporting these studies, and I am not a hypocrite. I have expertise in Death Studies, and I have experience with a dying spouse. Jordan Peterson's behaviour has been justified through the sickness of his wife. Therefore, let me answer back to this man and his hypocrisy. I am a white, heterosexual, academic woman. Jordan Peterson is a white, heterosexual, academic man. This is the moment to summon 'strategic binarism.' I am not denying a diversity of identities. But I am summoning these clean binary oppositions to demonstrate the power and injustices held within them. In *12 Rules,* Peterson stated, "Death shames the living."[25] Let us slip inside the shame and sit here a while. Let me tell a story of academic death.

My late husband was Professor Steve Redhead, Professor of Cultural Studies, founder of the Manchester Institute for Popular Culture, the man who created new disciplines in law, leisure, sport and philosophy. He wrote 17 books. We were married for 16 years. He died.

---

[23] I also wanted to note that there is, as Chelsey Hauge and Kate Reid confirmed, a "silencing of stories of cancer alterity," from "A production of survival: cancer politics and feminist media literacies," *Studies in Social Justice*, Vol. 13, No. 1, 2019, pp. 118–141. For non-binary individuals or trans citizens, there are few research projects and few places to express cancer narratives. Heteronormative stories of suffering and struggle dominate. I am aware that this Rule is heteronormative in its structure and reinforces this pattern. But it has been configured in this way to reduce the silence and suffering of women that 'manage' the death of their partners and to highlight the shocking proportion of heterosexual men that leave their wives during a terminal diagnosis. I welcome and acknowledge the presentation and dissemination of these other intricate and important stories of caring and loss from the LGBTQNI2+ communities.

[24] Noir (2020).

[25] Peterson (2018).

It all started normally. Well, normal for us, which was always pretty relative. Steve went yellow. There was no other signal that anything was wrong, worrying or problematic. One day, he turned a jaundice yellow. Unaware of the seriousness of this symptom, while organizing a doctor's appointment, I made Donovan jokes and sung "Mellow Yellow" and "Goodbye yellow brick road" throughout the day. After a sojourn through Dr Google, I'd ascertained he was suffering from gall stones. I was so wrong. The yellowing of the skin connoted the death sentence. After the diagnosis of pancreatic cancer, he lived for another eight months and died on March 8, 2018, at 12:20am. He died with me alone in the room—as was his choice.

When he was diagnosed, he wanted the illness to remain a secret between us until his death. No medical interventions. He wanted to stay at home, finish his book *Theoretical Times*,[26] conclude his other research projects and die on his own terms. Our relationship shifted and morphed immediately. Life had been taken away from this brilliant man. I had one remaining job. I had to return choice and agency to him during these final days.

When the worst happens, it is stunning how it is assumed through the excesses of neoliberalism that if we can all over-share, talk through our feelings and think positively, then the world will right itself. Steve was dying. He deserved space. He was a brilliant man. He could not choose an alternative to death. But he sure as hell could choose how he lived. He chose privacy. He chose supporting me as a dean at Flinders University in Adelaide, Australia. He chose finishing his research and dying in private. He gave me clear instructions about how to manage his life after his death. I did not want him defined by his illness. He was not pancreatic cancer. He lived as a scholar until he died. Steve had lived a life of theory. Death would continue his theories of disappearance. The pages of *Theoretical Times* are soaked in the language of disease, death, claustropolitanism, decay, denial, despair and pessimism. But no one knew or even suspected his illness. Steve played with digitization to remain present, even as he disappeared.

I looked after him at home without any medical intervention until the last three days. I maintained a full-time job as a woman, a professor and a dean. His secrecy about the illness was maintained until the night of his death. I then followed his instructions about how that death was to be revealed and managed.

Let me be life-affirmingly honest. Let me express what most of us repress or rarely have the context to share. The most alone any of us will ever feel is being alone in a room with our dead partner at the moment they left life. That is alone. That is the point when I had to weigh and measure how much of me died with him. There were no pharmaceuticals, rehab centres or long sabbaticals for me. I had to look death in the face, and somehow continue to live.

The day after Steve's death I returned to work. That was my responsibility. Work—particularly in peak capitalism—does not respect personal tragedy and our universities as a workplace are not geared or structured to manage a tragedy of this scale. There is no care for the carers. That is the point. I was a woman alone managing

---

[26] Redhead (2017).

the death of my husband in private, away from the Health Industrial Complex.[27] I managed his illness and his death, and I continue to carry his legacy. That is my responsibility. That is my burden. That is my gift.

There was no one I could lean on, rely on, there was no drugs to take to block out the pain, there was no safe tenured job to leave temporarily on full pay. I was a carer for a man I loved more than life, while in full time work. From this brutalizing experience, I have learned one thing with certainty.

Your partner's death is not about you.[28]

The privilege of escorting a spouse from life into death is deep and profound, and filled with horror and fear. In death, as in birth, there is no rehearsal. There is no practice. We experience both these events only once. For the carers of the dying, we give everything, we give of the deep self, wanting nothing in return, knowing our efforts, our love our attention will not create a happy ending. Our role—in the last months, weeks, days and hours—is to give agency to a person who has lost everything. Importantly Peterson was not prepared to do it. In the hour-long interview with his daughter, he only talked about himself. He had been away from his wife for much of her six months of recovery.[29] Is this a role model for a self-help guru?

It remains the greatest privilege of my life to have been married to Steve and to escort him to death. It is a horror movie that plays in my mind every day. But this sustained, enduring distress is not about me. There are millions of people walking this earth today who have lived this tragedy, this horror, this beauty and this peace, knowing that we cared for the dying and dead for no other reason but to respect the decency of human life, even when it ends.

This is not a story of individual choice and strength, but of collective kindness and meaning. With all the anger and nastiness of cancel culture and snowflakes, there is a denial of the place and value of those who care for fragile people as their clocks stop.[30] Our culture is filled with wounded people like me walking around the world. We cannot check out of the dread, the terror, the awkwardness, the fear and the loss.

---

[27] Steve chose a direct cremation. He never shared the reasons for this decision, perhaps because he wanted to reduce the intense stress on me. Perhaps he chose this because he died in Adelaide, Australia, which neither of us claimed as 'home.' We were living in the city to work. Therefore, this refusal to participate in a funeral was an important moment of negation. As Brian Parsons has confirmed, "the funeral is the ultimate rite of passage. It is a complex social drama in which performance and rituals are prescribed by social, religious and economic criteria together with personal preference," from *The evolution of the British funeral industry in the 20th Century: From Undertaker to Funeral Director*, (Bingley: Emerald, 2018), p 3. The funeral offers a time-specific response to death, by removing the dead from the living and generating a capitalist and controlled social interaction around a dead body.

[28] I note Sallie Tisdale's maxim: "your burden is yours to carry: don't ask a dying person to carry it for you," *Advice for future corpses (and those who love them): a practical perspective on death and dying*, (Crows Nest: Allena and Unwin, 2018), p. 126.

[29] "Peterson Family Update," *op. cit.*

[30] Sallie Tisdale's *Advice for future corpses (and those who love them): a practical perspective on death and dying*, (Crows Nest: Allena and Unwin, 2018) provides powerful advice for carers managing these debilitating and tragic circumstances.

We have to try and do the impossible, to keep on living, when every part of us wants to die. Therefore, it is appropriate to finish this Rule with two final stories.

First story. I am walking from the carpark up the hill to my office on Wednesday morning, July 29, 2020. A woman I knew by sight but not by name was just ahead of me. She turned and walked back to me. In my job, I always worry that someone is about to offer a complaint, but the woman said hello and started her sentence with a remarkable opening: "I've always wanted to tell you this, but a couple of years ago you helped me. My husband was very sick. I thought I might lose him. I was sitting over there, looking at the ocean, absolutely devastated and feeling sorry for myself. And I saw you walking up the hill in a red dress and smiling at me on the way up. And I thought if Tara can keep going. So can I." I asked her how her husband was going. She replied that he got better. I thanked her so much for her kind words and expressed relief that her husband had made it. These are the stories between women that are so often silent. Rarely told. We walk through the world wounded but surviving. That survival has its own story. It is a feminist story.[31]

My final story is about men. Or a man. To recycle the critique from Sky News, no I am not talking about all men. I am talking about high profile hypocrites, and also the men who decide to live differently. After Steve's death I tried to work out who I was without him. I survived. I rebuilt my life the best I could. There is no template or model for this. I had lost everything. I had to discover if I had any life left to live. Suddenly, I received an incredible gift. Another remarkable man entered my life: Professor Jamie Quinton. Because there are so few stories of men, women and death circulating in our culture, how exactly how do people create new spaces for a life after a death? Australian demography shows the challenges. Divorced people tend to have a far greater likelihood of remarriage than those who are widowed. Over half (56%) of men who divorce could expect to remarry, compared with 8% of remarriage among men who were widowed. For divorced women, 46% could expect to remarry. Just 3% of widowed women could expect to remarry.

Clearly, a lot is happening in this space of death when someone is still alive. To cite Derrida from his only scholarly monograph on Marx, "One must take another step. One must think of the future, that is, life. That is, death."[32] But with Peterson's focus on young men creating a heteronormative marriage, where are the alternative stories for men to understand and care for other men, other women, other people claiming different spaces beyond the binaries and transcending the assumed narratives of life?

We must make these narratives. We must build this vocabulary. These stories of death and loss are embarrassing and uncomfortable. Every individual who grieves, grieves alone. Jamie had to make his own way, park his individuality, his ego, and create a new space beyond what a Jordon Peterson could experience, research or express. This is how Jamie accomplished his dialogue with the dead, summoning a

---

[31] There are no happy endings to be offered in academic life. The university is a challenging workplace. Significantly, Alexander Clark and Bailey Sousa termed their book, *How to be a happy academic*, (Thousand Oaks: SAGE, 2018). Even with this title, the threats of corporatization, reduction in academic standards, bullying and high volumes of work are discussed as increasing the vulnerability of academic work and the institution.

[32] Derrida (1994).

language without shape, cadence or tone. One day he said to me—as we were trying to work out if and how we could create a present and future—"I've had a talk with Steve."

Just to clarify. Jamie never met Steve and I met Jamie ten months after Steve's death. From the discomfort, silence and confusion, he created a new space to respect Steve, respect me, and try to understand the past to create a future with the phrase, "I've had a talk with Steve."

These are the stories of real people, not snowflakes, not drama queens, not people suffering from severe spotlight deprivation, not men fighting like lobsters. Because… Because we cannot fight the dead. These are the stories of honest people who have lost—suffered—but had to continue to work and live. To continue to write. Helene Cixous stated that, "to begin (writing, living) we must have death. Writing is learning to die. It's learning not to be afraid, in other words, to live at the extremity of life, which is what the dead, death, gives us."[33] These devastatingly honest words cascade into stories, and they begin when we respect the sick, the dying and the dead.

The hypocrisy of Jordan Peterson must be named, labelled and understood. While instructing others how to be a man, his self-absorption and movement from mediocre professor to blow hard public commentator resulted in drug addiction and long stays in rehabilitation clinics. That is a personal tragedy, requiring support, care and understanding. However, this was not a personal story. This was a marketized public narrative that revealed the hypocrisy of his rules, slogans and advice. But the greatest tragedy of all is the speed at which he lost himself in addiction and put his needs ahead of his wife's challenges after she received the dreadful determination of a terminal illness. This behaviour must be recognized. He is not a self-help guru. He is a shadow of a man. He is weak. Yet even when logging his narcissism, his self-absorption, his disrespect and denial of the needs of others, he continues to teach men how to behave. This is self-help funnelled from the septic tank of life. He states in *Beyond Order: 12 More Rules for Life*, "the meaning that sustains people through difficult times is to be found not so much in happiness, which is fleeting, but in in (sic) the voluntary adoption of mature responsibility for the self and others."[34] He failed to abide by his own standards and rules. He was a man who could not manage the life he created and decentred his wife through her sickness. And yet. And yet. Jordan Peterson still has the gumption to discuss "the voluntary adoption of mature responsibility for self and others."[35] This is the equivalent of taking advice about vegan recipes from a butcher, or discussing Satan with the Pope. He failed to respect the sick. He lost himself in the selfishness of addiction. This is a personal tragedy, but a stark wake up call for the followers of this self-help expert.

This is a tough rule to write, but necessary. I did not have the luxury of drug use or rehabilitation. Most carers do not, because even after the death, the responsibilities, the loss, the horror and the death-anchored living continues. My husband died. I was the only one who could take care of him to his death. That was a responsibility and

---

[33] Cixous (2017).

[34] Peterson (2021).

[35] ibid., p. xxvi.

burden so heavy that it cannot be conveyed through language. Decent people—with 'mature responsibility'—face the horror of life without a crutch or support, because there is nothing available. We must work. We must care. We must survive so that another human can die with dignity. For all the people who have cared to the end of a life, who live those final images of death as a constant loop in their minds, we see Jordan Peterson for who he is. A man who—when death looked him in the eye—scurried away in fear. For the rest of us, we must feel the fear and act with compassion, even when there is no hope. That is the embodiment of courage.

References

Cixous, H. (2017). Three Steps on the ladder of writing. *School of the Damned*, p. 7. https://issuu.com/schoolofthedamned/docs/three-steps-cixous.

Cook, J. (2019). *Sustainability, human well-being, and the future of education.* Springer.

Derrida, J. (1994). *Specters of Marx: The state of the debt, the work of mourning and the new international* (p. 141). Routledge.

Fisher, A. (2019). A short history of serving the wholeness in each other. *Slug*, 114. https://expressmedia.org.au/product/voiceworks-114-slug/.

Glantz, M., Chamberlain, M., Liu, Q., Hsieh, C., Edwards, K., Van Horn, A., & Recht, L. (2009). Gender disparity in the rate of partner abandonment in patients with serious medical illness. *Cancer, 115*(22), 5237–5242.

Noir, P. (2020, 30 March). The men who leave their spouses when they have a life-threatening illness. *The Guardian.* https://www.theguardian.com/lifeandstyle/2020/mar/30/the-men-who-give-up-on-their-spouses-when-they-have-cancer.

Peterson, J. (2018). *12 rules for life* (p. 30). Penguin.

Peterson, J. (2021). *Beyond order: 12 more rules for life*, p. xxvi. London: Penguin.

Peterson, J. (2018). *12 rules for life.* Penguin.

Peterson, J., DeYoung, C., Driver-Linn, E., Seguin, J., & Higgins, D. (2003). Self-deception and failure to modulate responses despite accruing evidence of error. *Journal of Research n Personality, 37*(3), 205–223.

Peterson, J. (2021). *Beyond order: 12 more rules for life.* Penguin.

Reagle, J. (2015). *Reading the comments: Likers, haters, and manipulators at the bottom of the web.* MIT Press.

Redhead, S. (2017). *Theoretical times.* Emerald.

Chapter 13
Rule 12–Be the change you want to see

Mahatma Gandhi is frequently logged as the author of the title of this rule and chapter. That is not accurate. But Gandhi did confirm the importance of changing our inner world to activate transformations beyond our body. Sometimes, the greatest political action we can undertake is be present. To survive. To stand. The problem with Jordan Peterson's evangelical commitment is—as with so many preachers—he has been found out to be a hypocrite. If the currency is faith, worship, devotion and emulation, then the intellectual god must be worthy of this attention. Jordan Peterson is not.

What makes humans great - like Mahatma Gandhi - is not the strength and the victory and the fight and the violence, but the capacity to be vulnerable, to configure a language of weakness and share it with others. This is not a snowflake. This is not a keyboard warrior. This is a community that creates the space for debate and difference, but also kindness and compassion. We are judged by how we treat those who can be of no benefit to us. Instead, Jordan Peterson offers simple answers to questions about work, money, women, white people and America.

I have held back from speaking about Jordan Peterson for six years. Six years of reading and thinking. Six years of wide eyes in response to inelegant behaviour. Six years of shaking my head. Six years of tears for those hurt by his words. Six years of fear for those who follow him and believe that this is how life operates. Perhaps what this sad six years summons though is a question that feminists and progressives must answer. What constitutes a meaningful life? One answer is my final rule: be the change you want to see.

Our workplaces are ruthless.[1] The phrase peak capitalism tries to capture the extreme harm[2] and hazards created through the daily negotiation of life. We must create something different. We require workplaces, universities and families that leave spaces and creates places for the vulnerable, the grieving, the transitioning, the delicate. I want our culture to have those metaphoric kiosks that we see in airports,

---

[1] Schulte (2015).

[2] McRae (2018).

the charging stations that enable life's travellers to stop, from wherever we are in the world and wherever we are going, and recharge. It is free. It is generous. It is international. It is a space to repair and recharge whatever fixture or fitting we have. No desperation. I want a culture where all of us can walk past these recharge stations, these pockets of life, and feel without judgment, enact public mourning rituals as required, or sit quietly in private grief or thought.

Our workplaces—our leisure spaces—our universities—must be robust and compassionate, leaving spaces in the weave of learning to feel in ways that operate just at the edge of civility.[3] We are judged as individuals and as a university and as a culture by how we manage those precious people who need to walk a little more delicately through life for a while, perhaps clinging to the life raft of a degree, or who wake up in the morning uncertain if they want to continue living that day.

Jordan Peterson wanted men to "be the reliable person at a funeral."[4] He failed at that goal. Therefore, let us not think of reliability and funerals. Let us think of community and life. Our opportunity is to make universities—and life–like that recharge station at an airport. All sorts of different connections should be available: counselling or talk therapy if it helps, friendship, laughter, dancing or privacy. The person living in and with loss – which is all of us with different levels of intensity— must order their thoughts and desires the best they can, work out the relationship between public and private, and speak the words of what they want, and - most importantly - of what they do not want. Our task as an organic intellectual, if we choose to accept it, is to provide that recharging kiosk—that safe space—where a person can choose the connections that they need, sit in silence, but also rebuild and stay connected with important ideas and people.

Pain never goes away, but the pain is situated in different contexts. We can reflect on death and life, learning and ignorance, in different ways and from different perspectives. That—for me—is the definition of courage. And change.

References

McRae, L. (2018). *Terror, leisure and consumption: Spaces for harm in a post-crash era*. Emerald.
Peterson, J. (2017). Be the reliable person at the funeral. *Bite-size Philosophy YouTube Channel*, Retrieved form 12 June 2017, from https://www.youtube.com/watch?v=iDcOuTdjq8E
Shir-Wise, M. (2017). *Time freedom and the self: The cultural construction of 'free' time*. Palgrave.
Schulte, B. (2015). *Overwhelmed: How to work, love, and play when no one has the time*. Bloomsbury.

---

[3] Michelle Shir-Wise stated that, "When we think and talk about time, we relate to it as though it is tangible, something that we can spend, save or put away for another day. We treat it as a rare commodity as we do money. There never seems to be enough of it and what we have, is expected to be used wisely. Yet we are constantly afraid of wasting time so we attempt to regulate it in order to utilize it efficiently," from Shir-Wise (2017).

[4] Peterson (2017).

Chapter 14
Conclusion: Our future is in the post

The Jordan Peterson moment is over. We have entered a Post Peterson Paradigm. But the lessons learned for academics and our universities can now be audited. Empirical science is not the only available knowledge system. The validation of men in a suit summoning uneven research, funded by problematic individuals and corporations, cherry-picking from a skewed data set, must stop.

There are lessons to learn. We must consider why Jordan Peterson was popular, and recognize the damage he has enacted. He summoned an old-fashioned social order that appeared to value 'science' but actual validated selective and reified empiricism and 'clinical' experiences that are not generalizable. He was angry about the truncation of his free speech in the name of political correctness. But once the unicorns and wizards and other mythical creatures summoned through the mantras of 'free speech,' 'cancel culture' and 'political correctness' are revealed to be an illusion and ridiculous, scholars can research how the extreme right and left—although few in number—have revelled in a toxic choreography that has poisoned other social and intellectual movements. Slavoj Zizek described "the Alt-Right obsession with Cultural Marxism (Peterson's 'postmodern neo-Marxism')."[1] This obsession has resulted in an inelegant theorization of capitalism that has confused the market economy with free enterprise. Capitalism can and does have regulation and governance. Public policy ensures that our land, air and water are not poisoned, workers are able to earn a living in safety, and public education is valued—not as a commodity—but as part of citizenship. Instead, the freedom to live without fear of violence or the freedom to participate in a high-quality educational experience, or the fear of living without adequate health care are rarely discussed. Instead, freedom of speech becomes the freedom to be racist, sexist or homophobic without consequences. Kamala Harris once stated that "there is no vaccine for racism."[2] Similarly, there is no vaccine for ignorance. Peterson was evangelically committed to the supposed

---

[1] Zizek (2020).

[2] Harris (2020).

meritocracy that emerges through working hard, competing, being a strong individual and assuming responsibility. But we no longer live in the jewel box of Samuel Smiles' *Self-help*. The issue is that Peterson's wrongness, his errors, hypocrisy and flaws, speak to young men. There is a reason. Peterson believes in the patriarchy. He despises—without expertise or research—Marxism, feminism and postmodernism because they crack and shatter the foundations of patriarchy. He fights to sustain the natural order because – for an increasingly small group of people—they gain from it.[3] The cost of undermining public health has been seen through the diverse national responses to the COVID-19 pandemic. The nations that implemented regulated, coordinated responses controlled the outbreaks and minimized deaths. The nations celebrating individual rights to buy toilet paper and go to a restaurant suffered high mortality rates. George Monbiot offered an explanation of how this irrationality emerged. He sourced the origins to a fading commitment to education.

> What do we call the age we live in? It's no longer the information age. The collapse of popular education movements left a void filled by marketing and conspiracy theories … What clear social changes mark out our time from those that precede it? To me it's obvious. This is the Age of Loneliness.[4]

In this powerful statement, Monbiot offers an explanation for Jordan Peterson, without naming him. Education demands that we read, write, listen, interpret and think. With the 'collapse' of such systems, shopping and the QAnon Shaman crowd our vista. Through this irrationality, this breakdown in conversation and connection, a deep, dark and despairing loneliness emerges, punctuated by silence and shouting, self-medication and sleeping. Jordan Peterson offers simple answers to deep questions about injustice. But 'the system' will not be salved by nostalgia.

The 'natural' order activates privilege, inheritance, nepotism, cronyism and noblesse oblige. It also validates platitudes and decontextualized dribble. To quote from the *12 Rules*: "the soul of the individual eternally hungers for the heroism of genuine Being, and that the willingness to take on that responsibility is identical to the decision to live a meaningful life."[5] His path to a meaningful life is meaningless mantras. In this way, Donald Trump and Jordan Peterson were and are linked. Neither should have been taken seriously. Both monetized and weaponized their supposed persecution by the left, women, the LGBTQNI + communities, and the black community. They were tiny men who lived tiny lives. Peterson gave messages to young men to tidy their room, be well groomed, and don't rock the boat. As Dixon stated, "Jordan Peterson is the dumb person's idea of a smart person. He is not an intellectual phenomenon, but a cultural phenomenon."[6] Similarly Tabatha Southey described him as, "the stupid man's smart person."[7] I do not use the word 'dumb' or 'stupid,' as both maintain a history of oppression and disrespect, but ignorant is more effective.

---

[3] I note Axel Bruns point: "educators stand to lose their privileged position as expert practitioners and theorists in a user-led environment," from Bruns (2011).

[4] Monbiot (2017a).

[5] Peterson (2018).

[6] Dixon (2018).

[7] Southey (2017), Is Jordan Peterson the stupid man's smart person? - Macleans.ca.

Similarly, Donald Trump was the ignorant person's idea of a smart president. When ignorance, predatory capitalism and evangelical Christianity align, an end times apocalypse emerges against—let us list the folk devils - the state, feminists, secularism, postmodernism, Marxists, liberals or the left.[8] As with Trump's lost election, facts, reality and truths are debateable and inverted. Facts do not matter. Instead, all outcomes can be overturned on the basis of a mirage, untruths and deceit.

This is a powerful time to consider the meanings of masculinity. It is important to log the consequences of displacing these discussions of masculinity in favour of 'harpy sisters.' This displacement is well revealed in Jordan Peterson's discussion with Camille Paglia.

> Here's the problem. This is something my wife has pointed out, too. She said, 'Well, men are going to have to stand up for themselves.' But here's the problem. I know how to stand up to a man who has unfairly trespassed against me. The reason I know that is because the parameters for my resistance are quite well defined, which is we talk. We argue. We push. And then it becomes physical. If we move beyond the boundaries of civil discourse, we know what the next step is. That's forbidden in discourse with women. So I don't know. It seems to me that it isn't men that have to stand up and say, 'Enough of this,' even though that is what they should do. It seems to me that it's the sane women who have to stand up against their crazy sisters and say, 'look enough of that. Enough man-hating. Enough pathology. Enough bringing disgrace on us as a gender.' But the problem there, and then I'll stop my little tirade, is that most of the women I know who are sane are busy doing sane things. They're off. They have their career. They have their family. They're quite occupied, and they don't seem to have the time or maybe even the interest to go after their crazy harpy sisters.[9]

If any statement could be used to demonstrate the reification, the subjectivity, the irrationality, the labelling, the judgment, the lack of reading and the ignorance of Jordan Peterson, then this single paragraph completes the task. Firstly, the validation of men's physical responses to other men is justified and naturalized, rather than questioned. His wife's opinion is presented, as if generalizable and representative of all women. The nature of the critique of 'crazy harpy sisters' is unclear, but clusters around 'man-hating,' 'pathology,' and women bringing other women into 'disgrace.' What is clear is that 'sane' women, who have a career and a family and are 'occupied,' must patrol 'crazy harpy sisters' who—it seems—probe issues beyond the personal.

This is Jordan Peterson's view of women: the 'sane' women who accept their lot and the 'crazy harpy sisters' who question, critique, probe and challenge. If a man challenges another man, in Peterson's order, it can result in a physical altercation. If a woman is involved in a critique, then a man cannot 'get physical.' The reason for that differentiation is unclear, but the rates of domestic violence suggest that other men are not deploying that differentiation. But what is key in this statement is that the calm, quiet, hardworking, occupied women, supporting men and maintaining the system that demeans and undermines them is valued in Peterson's world view. As he states, "I don't see any regulating force for that terrible femininity, and it seems to me to be invading the culture and undermining the masculine power of the culture in what

---

[8] Toynbee and Walker (2017).

[9] Peterson (2017a).

I think is, fatal. I really do believe that."[10] In response to this 'terrible femininity,' it is clear that harpies of the world must unite. We have nothing to lose but our chains, and the respect of Jordan Peterson.

Is a focus on 'the self' anything more than selfish politics in a brutalizing time? Is the map of our meaning and personal development the most important projects for the world? When does an identity lens become a shutter? One answer to this question is that academics have not created the stories and the scaffolds to revision a new public sphere, confirming the value of reading widely and thinking deeply. George Monbiot stated that,

> You cannot take away someone's story without giving them a new one. It is not enough to challenge an old narrative, however outdated and discredited it may be. Change happens only when you replace it with another.[11]

Atomized, isolated and lonely citizens have chosen between the social democratic story of community and collective participation and the neoliberal story of individual choices and rights. Shopping has been chosen over belonging. It is easier to take a selfie and upload it to Facebook than to have a complex and intricate conversation about building beyond an atomized image of ourselves, with or without a filter.

Justifications for inequality are irrational and harmful. The fetishization of skin-based differences, a validation of particular higher powers over others, or over-reading and valuing particular folds of flesh that constitute genitals results in arbitrary, inconsistent and damaging hierarchies and justifications. The historical and continuing marginalization of women and feminine ideologies confirms this point.[12] Women are human. Women academics have a right to exist, to teach, to write, to be promoted, to be vice chancellor. Women have a right to be feminists. Women have a right to be anti-feminist. All citizens have a right to be anti-feminist. We have fought for our diversity through generations of women's history. But our role as feminists is to configure the alternative narratives, stories and histories that have been framed, demeaned and marginalized as gossip, popular culture or trash.

Nesrine Malik stated—flatly and powerfully—that "the social contract between the state and its female citizens is broken."[13] The catalogue of daily injustices that prick at women, the trans community, non-binary identifying citizens, and most men is clear. Reproductive rights are attacked, weathered and minimized. The gender pay gap remains. Trolling uses misogyny as its cooking oil. The fear of violence or redundancy in the streets, workplace or the home means that there is no capacity for women to stretch, to know what their best lives may be. For Peterson, his 'management' of women is dependent on behaviour and appearance. The checklist is clear. 'We' must not be a harpie. 'We' must not be radical. 'We' must support the gender and sexual order and be complicit in this ordering. This truncated vista results in women

---

[10] ibid.

[11] Monbiot (2017b).

[12] I note Derrida's (2020). He states, "The university is a system that, through its programs, assessments, and constraints, aims to ensure the re-production of is organization, which amounts not only to maintaining the system of forces but also to rigidifying the living being in death," p. 7.

[13] Malik (2019).

balancing caring and working responsibilities, a sexuality performed within finite and patrolled boundaries, and being educated only to work in areas that governmental policies undermine and minimize, such as health and education, and are therefore not paid well. Possessing a vagina grants magical powers for the capacity to cook and clean. Such meritocratic ideologies confirm that women are under-represented in the highest levels of government and business because they either do not work hard enough or are not bright or skilled enough.

Our task is to summon and remember those women that were labelled as harpies, shrill, nasty or—indeed stroppy. As feminists, we must do more. We ask why. Why are intelligent women labelled harpies? Why are successful and publicly engaged women termed nasty? Most importantly, who gains-who benefits-from the circulation of these labels? Most importantly, the Post Peterson Paradigm confirms what we have lost through the marginalization and minimization of Cultural Studies. I have moved through the last 30 years with a singular question: what the hell happened to Cultural Studies? What THE HELL happened to Cultural Studies? I date the decline from 1992, when Routledge published an enormous book titled—10 points for innovation here—*Cultural Studies*.[14] It was based on a conference held two years earlier. This was the moment when the United States appropriated Cultural Studies. The United States colonized Cultural Studies. This was the moment when the history of Cultural Studies before this conference was frozen, simplified, narrowed, limited, mythologized and rendered a canon.[15] The losses from academic life and public discourse were clear. Cultural Studies aligned everyday life with the political economy. Scholars offered sharp and precise commentary in tough times. The loss of this razor of a paradigm was logged by Alain Badiou,[16] Graeme Turner[17] and— ironically although he did not see the irony—Laurence Grossberg.[18] Yet we see through the Jordan Peterson moment of fame, the cost of its decline.

Cultural Studies, as a post-disciplinary field, holds a radical history without apology. It is a history of the present but understands the past. It places texts into context, and the semiotic within the social semiotic. Most significantly, Cultural Studies scholars operate a switchblade to hypocrisy and injustice. The loss of Cultural Studies of its time and for its time is one of the reasons that Jordan Peterson was able to gain a profile without a systematic critique, and then proliferate that profile.

Cultural Studies has been stuck in this 1992 moment. We are now in the 2020s. Fine scholars mostly outside of Cultural Studies have written tremendous and inno- vative scholarship. Meanwhile, Cultural Studies has stayed in this freeze-dried 1992 moment. There has been some pretence to enact the 'political economy' through reifications of the creative industries. This term signifies high culture, with a bit

---

[14] Grossberg et al. (1992).

[15] An example of this 'frozen' paradigm, where Cultural Studies theories were traded for identity politics is Sandoval (2000).

[16] Badiou (2013).

[17] Turner (2012).

[18] Grossberg (2010).

of popular music and gaming on the side. Popular culture has never been more interesting. Popular Cultural Studies have never been more boring.[19]

Jordan Peterson emerged and Cultural Studies researchers were silent. Cultural Studies scholars could have made a difference. Fake News. Post Truth. Donald Trump. This freeze-dried Cultural Studies ignored the incredible scholarship, particularly from indigenous researchers, that blows the roof off theorizations of England in the 1970s and 1980s. Clearly, the world has changed. Scholarship has changed. Cultural Studies should have changed.

It did not. It failed.

What if Cultural Studies continues to drift into this imagined past? We have seen the results on this planet when the brightest minds lose the capacity to engage with daily life and popular culture because of limited reading,[20] gatekeeping of writing, little research funding without corporate strings, arbitrary metrics of publishing, and a lack of courage in the spirit of careerism. The assumption that North America was and is the centre of humanities thinking is also part of the Jordan Peterson critique. Most observed in his discussion with Camille Paglia,[21] the idea of French theory and theorists is dismissed with xenophobic recoil. Just as COVID-19 became the China Virus, so did intricate research become French theory. For both Paglia and Peterson, structuralism, poststructuralism, modernism, postmodernism and deconstruction[22] are collapsed into "French thought." Not only are all of these paradigms, theories and tropes different from each other, but each term has a delicate, intricate, complex and iterative history. To fuse and crush these refined intellectual trajectories into straw theories written by straw scholars is inelegant. As there was no evidence to verify Paglia and Peterson's interpretations, "techniques of neutralization"[23] were deployed through their video, confirming their views with the phrase, "everyone knows this."[24] 'Everyone' does not know or agree that Marxism, structuralism, poststructuralism or deconstruction are confluent, correct or incorrect. Instead, English speaking academics such as Paglia and Peterson are not prepared to enact the heavy lifting and show intellectual generosity to consider difficult, dense and challenging ideas. For example, the relationship between Derrida and Althusser requires careful analysis. If Derrida had Marxist moments, then it is through Althusserian Marxism.[25] Indeed, in perhaps the most bizarre of the errors summoned by Peterson, not only is postmodernism different from Marxism, but both are distinct from identity politics.

---

[19] I note my emerging correctives in Popular Cultural Studies. Please refer to Brabazon (2021) and with Elisa Armstrong (2020).

[20] The reification of scholarship has emerged in Parfitt's (2021). A bizarre book, Parfitt attempts to argue—and fails—in aligning Jordan Peterson and Adolf Hitler. Odd analyses emerge such as, "In order to understand Peterson, I've had to learn how to think like him. So will you," p. 56.

[21] Paglia and Peterson (2017).

[22] Deconstruction is significant in the history of ideas because it granted phenomenological perspectives a relativist ending or conclusion through theory.

[23] Sykes and Matza (1957).

[24] Paglia and Peterson, op. cit.

[25] There was also a personal relationship between Althusser and Derrida, with Derrida visiting Althusser in the clinic near Paris after he killed his wife.

The confusion of Marxism and postmodernism by Peterson reached the level of farce in the following statement.

> The force that's driving the activism is mostly the Marxism rather than the postmodernism. It's more like an intellectual gloss to hide the fact that a discredited economic theory is being used to fuel an educational movement and to produce activists. But there's no coherence to it.[26]

Therefore, the complete absence of Cultural Studies scholars from the critical responses to the Jordan Peterson 'moment' is important. At its best, Cultural Studies separates these intellectual and political tendencies with precision and care. This was the gift of Cultural Studies. As Carl Bergstrom and Jevin West argued, "the amount of energy needed to refute bullshit is an order of magnitude bigger than that needed to produce it."[27] Yet, as shown by the Jordan Peterson moment, if the silliness, hyperbole and inaccuracies are allowed to continue and expand, it becomes almost impossible to stop the evangelical commitment to the chimera, error and flaws. It also becomes much more difficult to affirm the importance of information and media literacy,[28] reading a diversity of complex and intricate sources and persisting to interpret, analyse and balance a diversity of views.

There were moments of warning and foreshadowing. In *Maps of Meaning*, his first scholarly monograph published in 1999, he confirmed that 'culture' was his focus.

> Something we cannot see protects us from something we do not understand. The thing we cannot see is culture, in its intrapsychic or internal manifestation. The thing we do not understand is the chaos that gave rise to culture. If the structure of culture is disrupted, unwittingly, chaos returns. We will do anything—anything—to defend ourselves against that return.[29]

It is important to consider how 'culture' is deployed in this passage. It is a proxy for communication systems, context, the environment, history and change. That is a provisional list. Significantly this culture that creates 'chaos' is "intrapsychic" or an "internal manifestation." In other words, 'culture' has been used with such ambiguity and vagueness that it is meaningless, almost as meaningless as the use of the word 'chaos.'

We can do better. Cultural Studies scholars are students with their origins in the research of Raymond Williams.[30] His legacy and influence must undergird our teaching and our research. His legacy confirmed that culture was and is outward. Activated. Actualized. Williams lived a magisterial career, encased in the imperative to connect daily life with social change. Peterson picked on Lacan, Foucault and Derrida. Althusser, Poulantzas and Anderson – Perry Anderson[31] although Benedict

---

[26] Peterson (2019).

[27] Bergstrom and West (2020).

[28] Brabazon (2011).

[29] Peterson (1999).

[30] To sample his remarkable legacy, please refer to Williams (1963, 1965 and 1973).

[31] I recognize Perry Anderson's strong theorization of periodization and postmodernism. He stated, "postmodernism emerged as a cultural dominant in unprecedently rich capitalist societies with very high average levels of consumption," Anderson (1998).

may have also been an informative scholar - would have been more worthwhile oppo-
nents. Significantly the research of women—whether Butler, Cixous or Irigaray—
was absent. The powerful Australian intellectual Marcia Langton, who changed
so many of our lives, is beyond his comprehension and bibliography. Indigenous
methodologies matter and are transformative of all knowledge systems. Colonization, dispossession and injustice require active and interventionist strategies. Without
overt and conscious methods to manage change, injustices are normalized.

Instead, the focus is on academic freedom, with an entrée into racist and sexist
speech. Such arguments are valued as critiquing cancel culture and "cultures of
safetyism."[32] The great question is if students in universities should confront ideas
that undermine their identity. This is not identity politics. This is a question as to
whether a student has a right to learn, rather than defend their right to exist. If a student
is confronting abuse about their identity, then they are not reading or writing. The
question is why the focus is on the self rather than learning beyond the self. Writers
such as Peterson, and Greg Lukiannof and Jonathan Haidt, in their *The coddling of
the American Mind*,[33] confuse the learning of diverse histories, literatures, languages
and cultures with emotions and identity politics, rather than rigour and empirical and
theoretical complexity. EH Carr stated in 1961 that "history means interpretation."[34]
Only particular facts have survived in our present. Therefore, assuming that the
source material—the material culture—that remains in our present is accurate, true
and convincing while alternative interpretations are emotional or intuitive perpetuates
a misunderstanding of history, information literacy and knowledge.

Actually, high theory and the humanities encourage deep and complex thinking.
This is not safe knowledge. It is tough, rigorous and difficult. Through the polariza-
tion of debates since Margaret Thatcher and Ronald Reagan, but intensified since
September 11,[35] there has been a need for conservative forces to summon a singular,
universal real that is safe, nostalgic and obviously—imaginary. If a singular version
of history, truth and reality can be constructed, then that is comforting for the groups
in power.[36] This singular lens deflects attention from the injustices of colonization
that continue to live and breathe and maim. This singular lens displaces attention on
poverty, that continues to cannibalize the childhoods of generation after generation,
or where women are still not entitled to equal pay for equal work or recognition
of the economic value of care. This singular reality celebrates and pays for STEM,
while the caring professions that add decency and light to the lives of the very young
and the very old, remain underpaid and casualized. This singular reality erases the

---

[32] Lukianoof and Haidt (2018).

[33] Ibid.

[34] Carr (1963).

[35] I note Bennett (2019). She confirms the re-emergence of narratives about heroic masculinity and
the women requiring protection and rescuing.

[36] As James Ball confirmed, "we're all inclined to ... look for and accept information which supports
our current beliefs," from Ball (2017), p. 180.

lives and systems securing rights and meaning for the trans community and non-binary identifying citizens. It refuses space and a voice for those attempting to transform assumptions about heteronormative procreation. Yet instead of recognizing the flawed premise, that there is not a singular interpretation of the meaningful or the right or the real, the "Postmodern NeoMarxists"[37] or 'the media'[38] are blamed for 'creating' this crisis in reality. Therefore, blame and attack is summoned against those offering alternatives. Actually this 'crisis' is configured so that unemployment, violence, poverty, the Global Financial Crisis, war, the death of millions of people through a pandemic that could have been controlled through a commitment to public health, and environmental destruction, is blamed on individuals rather than revealing the corrosive, deadening structures of our lives. Indeed, instead of exploring these structural and often catastrophic events, Jordan Peterson creates what David Dennen has described as "crisis autobiography."[39]

Crises hold a function in political narratives. Crises pause, stop and freeze more progressive, gradual and considered policy developments and movements. They are a moment of metaphoric fire that burns the pretty branches and peaceful surfaces of carefully configured change. But after these crises burn, we can see the resultant death, blackness, decay and vulnerability with clarity and precision. As Hall, Critcher, Jefferson, Clarke and Roberts argued in 1978—through *Policing the Crisis*—the crisis is not a crisis.[40] The crisis maintains a key function in creating 'the true' and 'the real.' The issue is not the representation of women, non-binary identifying people, indigenous communities or communities of colour. The representation is—to be frank—just a representation. But a crisis triggered by the representation of war, riots, health, sickness, protests or violence perpetuates particular versions of truth and reality. The real and the true are not threatened by the 'crises' of identity politics, cancel culture or political correctness. The crisis is invented to shape and configure a version of reality that blocks dialogue, conversation and debate.

This focus on crisis is not an emotional rendering of variable circumstances. Our time requires attention to the political economy. Trauma is subjective. But this subjectivity does not invalidate its existence. The imperative must be to lift the standards and scope of reading, writing and thinking, avoiding generalizations, labelling and the substitution of emotion for interpretation. Intriguingly, scholars attacking 'cancel culture' or 'identity politics' demonstrate their lack of epistemological expertise through their simplification of methodologies and ontologies. The problem is not freedom of speech. The problem is ignorance. The problem is science conducted by press release. The problem is politics conducted by the size of the political donation. The problem is the proliferation of low-quality information disconnected from evidence, argument and debate. Indeed, Bertrand Russell confirmed why writers commit to the true as a singular formation.

---

[37] Peterson (2017b).

[38] I note Overall and Nicholls (2020).

[39] Dennen (2019).

[40] Hall et al. (1978).

For pragmatism, a belief is 'true' if its consequences are pleasant ... In this way theories become instruments not answers to enigmas ... Truth is one species of good, not a separate category ... In other words, our obligation to speak truth is part of our general obligation to do what pays.[41]

Just as Trump played with the presidency like a frat boy opening a beer keg, Peterson played with argument and knowledge, lacking the reading, the research, and the international expertise. They used the same techniques: labelling, name calling, divisiveness, and summoning freedom of speech while silencing others. Both revealed profound problems with women. All their arguments cascade to dust if we acknowledge one truth. Women are fully human, with rights, with a room of our own, with the capacity to grow, make decisions, make mistakes, contribute to citizenship and public debate, speak, maintain rights over their body and breathe. If these truths are self-evident, then all the hyperbole about pussy grabbing, nasty women, radical feminists or harpies, disappears.

Jordan Peters stated that, "there is nothing more dangerous than a weak man."[42] Actually, there is nothing more dangerous than establishing false or imprecise binaries that rank humans into a hierarchy.[43] How is the separation of weak and strong men enabling for a diversity of masculine narratives, choices and decisions? But in a dreadful pot-kettle-black moment, within two years of making this statement, Jordan Peterson was not strong enough to avoid addiction to anti-anxiety drugs, prescribed because he could not manage the reality of his wife's illness. His addiction became the focus of the tale and his next publicity cycle.

Women are human. If there are citizens in our culture who wish women to be lesser, secondary, pushed aside, in support, silent, then Trump and his mode of leadership will continue for decades after his failed, single term presidency. Peterson and his mode of scholarship will be sustained if citizens continue to demand simple answers to the wrong questions. He validates traditional narratives about work, money, women, white people and North America that ignore the Global Financial Crisis and the profound impact of neoliberalism on learning, teaching, speaking, listening and living. As Conrad Bongard Hamilton argued so effectively,

Peterson's approach will seem immediately familiar: identify a social problem, often with a high degree of acuity, then – in lieu of a meaningful sociological analysis – propose as a solution the thing that caused the problem in the first place. Not enough women in certain sectors of the workforce? Maybe that's just because women are intrinsically different, and we should probably drop this demagogic push for equality altogether.[44]

To offer analysis, interpretation, and context is not a denial of truth, but an imperative to research, and demonstrate rigour, transparency, accountability and repeatability. For our difficult future, scholars are best placed to probe what Derrida described

---

[41] Russell (1910).

[42] J. Peterson, "Modern Times with Camille Paglia and Jordan Peterson," op. cit.

[43] The culture wars are normally considered to be underpinned by a confrontational binary. These can be seen in binaries such as liberal/conservative, left/right, socialist/capitalist, Democrat/Republican and so on", from Anthony (2020).

[44] Hamilton (2020).

as "a radical experience of the perhaps."[45] Focussing on this 'perhaps' allows scholars and citizens to recognize that if the cost of increasing individual rights—to speak, to shoot guns, to buy toilet paper, to have a haircut during a pandemic, to consume without consequences - i s he loss of rights in others, then that price is too high. By summoning this 'perhaps,' the very old debates can be parked that assume that the success of girls and women in schools, universities and the workplace as somehow retracting the life narratives of men. Women's achievements do not block men's achievement. Success is not a finite pie to be eaten. Success is contextual and can configure options and vistas beyond our primary socialization, if we listen, respect others, and take risks.

The profound oddity is, for all Peterson's attack on postmodernism, he is what he decries. He is the postmodern academic. Surviving on the floating signifiers of a conservative haircut, a sharp suit, a gender ambivalent voice, and Punch and Judy anger and fire, he is an academic without the background for academic credibility. Yes, like so many mediocre men, he gained an elite education in elite institutions and did not leave those elite institutions until he chose to resign. Jordan Peterson is the academic required for a generation that does not read, does not think, but wishes to watch a video and feel better. He is the veneer academic, presenting surfaces of credibility and gravitas, for a generation that does not want to research the experience of others, but wishes to sit in self-saturated confusion and disgust that the world does not revolve around them. What is fascinating from his fans, is there is a profound disinterest in his actual ideas, and the gap between his expressed ideas and the life he lives. A self-help writer only has the self, a big, bold, charismatic, self-absorbed, hyper-confident identity from which to offer evidence. Jordan Peterson does not have academic credibility, as confirmed by his peer reviewed scholarship, and he does not have the supernova self and connected narrative required for a self-help 'guru' such as Tony Robbins. Instead, we are left with a few apologist crumbs, such as Daniel Burston's comment that "few of Peterson's critics gave him any credit for good intentions."[46] Let us take this as a legitimate question. What are these good intentions? What could they be? The banal answers to such questions include, recentring the value of the individual, reminding citizens about the importance of freedom, and validating the masculine over the feminine. These are self-evident mantras of neoliberalism, most conservative ideologies, many religious organizations, self-help leaders and empowered institutions.

What is lost through such a narrative is remembering the value of an institution much larger and bigger than an individual and their choices, hopes and ambitions. Universities undergird the history of contemporary humanity. Almost all of the knowledge created in the last one hundred years emerged either from a university, or researchers trained within it.[47] As widening participation policies emerged through the 1990s, the rapid growth in student numbers meant that quality and quantity in the assessment of research and teaching quality started to blur. The arrival of performance

---

[45] Derrida (1994).

[46] Burston (2019).

[47] Bourner et al. (2020).

indicators and research and teaching measurement, such as the Research Assessment Exercise, the Research Excellence Framework and the Teaching Excellence Framework, started to summon new goals including graduate employability and work-ready graduates. Through this blurring and merging of purposes, the key goal—the advancement of knowledge—is being lost through short termism and credentialling. Jordan Peterson's attacks on the humanities are an attack on debate, reading, writing and research dissemination. His experience as a clinical psychologist configures a distinct and limited alignment of methodology, ontology and epistemology. Other choices and modes in the development of knowledge are possible. Comprehensive universities span from engineering and the experimental sciences through to fine art and design. That is their gift. That diversity of knowledge is the true value of higher education. When we lose this scope and scale, knowledge becomes information and scholars become knowledge workers.

An intellectual does not accept the platitudes of fans, or the panderings of politically virulent forces. The great scholar challenges, pokes and probes their readers, listeners and colleagues to look in the mirror, read their own history and ponder their own mistakes and errors. More significantly, the great scholar demands that personal experience is not enough. Peterson reinforces the blame that young white heterosexual men place on women, gay, lesbian and trans communities, migrants and citizens of colour. He reinforces the historic orders of oppression, attacking those who wish to alleviate the social burdens on others. Great scholars open up debates, enter contexts of historic tragedy and create cultures of reflection, revision and re-evaluation. Jordan Peterson is Chauncie (the) Gardener of academic life. Like that late, great character from Peter Sellers in *Being There*,[48] those around him confuse banality, simplicity and literal statements with profundity, complexity and metaphors. The lack of reflection on his statements is the foundation for his popularity, while using populist techniques.[49]

The #metoo movement and Black Lives Matter are important. They are not ignoring men's rights or white people's rights. Saving the whales does not mean killing the dolphins. Jordan Peterson presents very simple ideas in a dreadful, conflictual, chaotic time. He is vanilla ice-cream after a long and difficult day. But he is still vanilla ice-cream, filled with sugar, preservatives and if we consume too much, it will create brain freeze. We are now in a Post Peterson Paradigm. The pointless intensity is in the past. We have a choice to read and think and dance and create space. This time, let's make that choice.

---

[48] *Being There*, (United Artists, 1979).

[49] I particularly note Joseph Harris and his argument that "intellectuals almost always write in response to the work of others." Jordan Peterson—through his lack of references and referencing – summons phrases such as 'most people,' 'feminists,' 'professors' rather than completing the detailed research required to create the force and weight of evidence. Please refer to Harris (2017).

References

Anthony, M. (2020). Web wide warfare: The Blue Shadow. *Journal of Futures Studies, 24*(4), 35–50.

Anderson, P. (1998). *The origins of postmodernity* (p. 121). Verso.

Armstrong, E., and Brabazon, T. (2020). Memes to a darker shade: Dark Simpsons, Un/popular culture and summoning theories of darkness. *International Journal of Social Sciences & Educational Studies, 7*(4). https://ijsses.tiu.edu.iq/wp-content/uploads/2020/12/Memes-to-A-Darker-Shade-Dark-Simpsons-UnPopular-Culture-and-Summoning-Theories-of-Darkness.pdf

Badiou, A. (2013). *Philosophy and the Event*. Polity.

Ball, J. (2017). *Post-Truth: How bullshit conquered the world* (p. 180). Biteback.

Bergstrom, C., & West, J. (2020). *Calling bullshit: The art of scepticism in a data-driven world*. Penguin.

Bennett's, E. (2019). *Gender in Post-9/11 American Apocalyptic TV: Representations of masculinity and femininity at the end of the world*. Bloomsbury Academic.

Bourner, T., Rospiglioi, A., & Heath, L. (2020). *The fully functioning university*. Emerald.

Brabazon, T. (2011). Take the red pill: building a matrix of literacies. *The Journal of Media Literacy Education, 2*(3). http://jmle.org/index.php/JMLE/article/view/112/90

Brabazon, T. (2021). Claustropolitanism, capitalism and Covid: Deviant leisure, un/popular culture, and a (post)work future. *International Journal of Social Sciences and Educational Studies, 8*(1), 57–73. https://ijsses.tiu.edu.iq/wp-content/uploads/2021/03/Claustropolitanism-Capitalism-and-Covid-UnPopular-Culture-at-the-End-of-the-World.pdf

Bruns, A. (2011). Beyond difference: Reconfiguring education for the user-led age. In: Land, R., & Bayne, S. (Eds). *Digital Difference: Perspectives on online learning* (p. 133). Sense Publishers.

Burston, D. (2019). 12 Rules for life. *Journal of Analytical Psychology, 64*(1), 105–111.

Carr, E. H. (1963). *What is History?* Penguin.

Dennen, D. (2019). Politics and prophecy: Jordan Peterson's antidote to modernity. *AS Journal Org, 66*.

Derrida, J. (1994). *Specters of Marx: The state of debt, the work of mourning and the New International* (p. 42). Routledge.

Derrida, J. (2020). *Life death*. University of Chicago Press.

Dixon, J. (2018). *Clean up your room! The eternal spotless mind of Jordan Peterson* (p. 1124). Nova Books.

Grossberg, L. (2010). *Cultural studies in the future tense*. Duke University Press.

Grossberg, L., Nelson, C., & Treichler, P. (Eds.). (1992). *Cultural Studies*. Routledge.

Hall, S., Critcher, C., Jefferson, M., Clarke, J., & Roberts, B. (1978). *Policing the Crisis: Mugging, the State, and Law and Order*. Macmillan.

Hamilton, C. (2020). Two pills, one cup: Late capitalism and the rise of neomasculinity. In M. McManus (Ed.), *What is postmodern conservatism: Essays on our hugely tremendous times* (p. 40). Zero books.

Harris, J. (2017). *Rewriting: How to do things with texts* (p. 1). Utah State University Press.

Harris, K. (2020). There is no vaccine for racism. *BBC News*. August 20, 2020, https://www.bbc.com/news/av/world-us-canada-53844453

Lukianoof, G., & Haidt, J. (2018). *The coddling of the American Mind: How good intentions and bad ideas are setting up a generation for failure* (p. 85). Penguin.

Malik, N. (2019). *We need new stories: Challenging the toxic myths behind our age of discontent* (p. 10). Weidenfeld and Nicolson.

Monbiot, G. (2017a). *How did we get into this mess?* (p. 9). Verso.

Monbiot, G. (2017b). *Out of the wreckage: A new politics for an age of crisis*. Verso.

Overall, R., & Nicholls, B. (2020). *Post-Truth and the Mediations of Reality: New conjunctures*. Springer.

Paglia, C., & Peterson, J. (2017). Modern Times with Camille Paglia and Jordan Peterson. *YouTube*. October 3, 2017, https://www.youtube.com/watch?v=v-hIVnmUdXM

Parfitt, T. (2021). *The devil and his due: how Jordan Peterson plagiarizes Adolf Hitler*. Western Hemisphere Press.

Peterson, J. (1999). *Maps of meaning: The architecture of belief* (p. xi). Routledge.

Peterson, J. (2017a). In: Paglia, C., & Peterson, J. (Eds) Modern Times with Camille Paglia and Jordan Peterson. *YouTube*. Retrieved October 3, 2017, from https://www.youtube.com/watch?v= v-hIVnmUdXM

Peterson, J. (2017b). Postmodern Neomarxism: Diagnosis and cure. *YouTube*. July 10, 2017, https:// www.youtube.com/watch?v=s4c-jOdPTN8.

Peterson, J. (2018). *12 Rules for life* (p. xxxiv). Penguin.

Peterson, J. (2019). The fatal flaw lurking in American leftist politics. *Big Think*. Retrieved January 1, 2019, from https://bigthink.com/videos/top-10-jordan-peterson-leftist-liberal-politics.

Russell, B. (1910). *"Pragmatism", Edinburgh Review, April 1909; reprinted in Philosophical Essays* (p. 121). Cambridge University Press.

Sandoval, C. (2000). *Methodology of the oppressed*. University of Minnesota Pres.

Southey, T. (2017). Is Jordan Peterson the stupid man's smart person? *Maclean's*. Retrieved November 17, 2017.

Sykes, G., & Matza, D. (1957). Techniques of Neutralization: A Theory of Delinquency. *American Sociological Review, 22*(6), 664–670.

Toynbee, P., & Walker, D. (2017). *Dismembered: How the attack on the state harms us all*. Guardian Books.

Turner, G. (2012). *What's become of cultural studies?* SAGE.

Williams, R. (1963). *Culture and society*. Columbia University Press.

Williams, R. (1965). *The long revolution*. Penguin.

Williams, R. (1973). *Communications*. Penguin.

Zizek, S. (2020). Jordan Peterson as a symptom of … What? In: Burgis, B., Hamilton, C., McManus, M., Trejo, M. (Eds). *Myth and Mayhem: A leftist critique of Jordan Peterson* (p. 2). Zero Books.